LIPARI

TRAVEL GUIDE

Lipari Uncovered: Your Comprehensive Guide to Italy's Stunning Aeolian Island

MICHAEL Z. WILSON

Copyright ©2024 Michael Z. Wilson

All rights reserved.

Unauthorized reproduction, distribution or use of this content is strictly prohibited without the prior knowledge or written permission of the copyright owner.

TABLE OF CONTENTS

WELCOME TO LIPARI 15

BRIEF HISTORY AND CULTURAL SIGNIFICANCE OF LIPARI 17
CLIMATE AND BEST TIME TO VISIT LIPARI 20
- The Best Time to Visit Lipari 22
- Weather Considerations and Tips 23

HOW TO GET TO LIPARI 25

BY AIR 25
BY TRAIN 26
BY FERRY OR HYDROFOIL 26
BY PRIVATE BOAT OR YACHT 28

GETTING READY FOR YOUR TRIP TO LIPARI 31

- Booking Travel and Accommodation 31
- Planning Activities and Itineraries 31
- Understanding Local Customs and Language 32
- Health and Safety Considerations 32

TRAVEL DOCUMENTS AND VISA REQUIREMENTS FOR LIPARI 33
- Passports and Identification 34
- Visa Requirements 34
- Travel Insurance 35
- Customs and Entry Procedures 36
- Important Considerations 36

CURRENCY, BANKING, AND BUDGETING TIPS FOR LIPARI 38
- Currency Overview 38
- Banking Services on Lipari 38
- Budgeting Tips for Your Trip to Lipari 39
- Money-Saving Tips 41

iii | Page

PACKING GUIDE: WHAT TO BRING TO LIPARI 43
- Clothing Essentials 43
- Beach and Water Gear 44
- Electronics and Travel Gadgets 44
- Health and Hygiene Items 45
- Travel Documents and Essentials 46
- Miscellaneous Items 47
- Seasonal and Activity-Specific Items 47

NAVIGATING LIPARI 49

- Using Public Transport 49
- Renting Vehicles 49
- Walking and Biking 50
- Boating Options 50
- Taxi Boats 51

TRANSPORTATION OPTIONS IN LIPARI: BUSES, TAXIS, AND CAR RENTALS 51
- Buses: A Cost-Effective and Convenient Choice 51
- Taxis: Flexible and Convenient 52
- Car Rentals: Freedom to Explore at Your Own Pace 53

WALKING AND BIKING ROUTES IN LIPARI 54
- Walking Routes: Discover Lipari on Foot 55
- Biking Routes 56
- Tips for Walking and Biking in Lipari 58

FERRY SERVICES TO NEIGHBORING ISLANDS: EXPLORING THE AEOLIAN ARCHIPELAGO 59

ACCOMMODATION OPTIONS 63

TYPES OF ACCOMMODATION 63
LUXURY HOTELS AND RESORTS IN LIPARI 63
- Top Luxury Hotels and Resorts 63
- Luxury Experiences and Services 66

BOUTIQUE HOTELS AND BED & BREAKFASTS IN LIPARI 68
- Boutique Hotels 68

BED & BREAKFASTS 70
- Choosing the Right Boutique Hotel or B&B 72
- Booking Tips 73

BUDGET ACCOMMODATION AND HOSTELS IN LIPARI 73
- Budget Hotels..73
- Hostels 75
- Guesthouses 76
- Tips for Budget Travelers in Lipari..77
- Making the Most of Your Budget Stay 78

CAMPING AND ALTERNATIVE STAYS IN LIPARI 78
- Camping in Lipari 79
- Alternative Stays: Unique Accommodations for a Memorable Experience..80
- Considerations for Camping and Alternative Stays..............83
- Making the Most of Your Alternative Stay..............................84

BOOKING PLATFORMS 84
- Local and Specialty Platforms..85
- Apps for Last-Minute Bookings 85
- Comprehensive Travel Apps 85

MUST-SEE ATTRACTIONS IN LIPARI: HIGHLIGHTS OF THE ISLAND 87

LIPARI CASTLE 87
- Visitor Information..88

MUSEO ARCHEOLOGICO REGIONALE EOLIANO 91
- The Museum's Layout and Sections..92
- Special Exhibits and Events..94
- Visitor Information..95

SPIAGGIA DI CANNETO..97
- Facilities and Amenities...99

v | Page

- Best Time to Visit 101
- Tips for Visitors 102

QUATTROCCHI VIEWPOINT 103
- Panoramic Views from Quattrocchi 103
- Getting to Quattrocchi Viewpoint 105
- Photography Tips for Quattrocchi Viewpoint 106
- Nearby Attractions 107
- Tips for Visiting Quattrocchi Viewpoint 108

CHURCHES AND RELIGIOUS SITES IN LIPARI: SAN BARTOLOMEO AND MORE 108
San Bartolomeo Cathedral *109*
OTHER NOTABLE CHURCHES AND RELIGIOUS SITES IN LIPARI 111
- Church of the Immaculate Conception 111
- Church of San Giuseppe 112
- Church of San Pietro 113

CHURCH OF SANTA CATERINA 114

EXPLORING NATURE IN LIPARI 117

HIKING TRAILS AND SCENIC WALKS IN LIPARI 118
- Overview of Lipari's Hiking Experience 118

TOP HIKING TRAILS IN LIPARI 119
- Monte Sant'Angelo Trail 119
- Quattrocchi Viewpoint Trail 120
- Monte Guardia Trail 121
- Acquacalda to Porticello Coastal Walk 122
- Lipari Archaeological Walk 123
- Tips for Hiking in Lipari 123

BOAT TOURS AND ISLAND HOPPING IN LIPARI 124
- Overview of Boat Tours in Lipari 124

POPULAR ISLAND-HOPPING DESTINATIONS FROM LIPARI 126
1. Vulcano *126*
2. Salina *127*

- 3. Panarea *128*
- 4. Stromboli *128*
- 5. Filicudi and Alicudi *129*
  - Practical Tips for Boat Tours and Island Hopping 130
- SNORKELING AND DIVING SPOTS IN LIPARI 130
  - Overview of Snorkeling and Diving in Lipari 131
- TOP SNORKELING AND DIVING SPOTS IN LIPARI 132
- 1. Pietra del Bagno *132*
- 2. Grotta del Cavallo *133*
- 3. Secca di Capistello *133*
- 4. Porticello Beach *134*
- 5. Punta Castagna *134*
- DIVING CENTERS AND SNORKELING TOURS 135
  - Practical Tips for Snorkeling and Diving in Lipari 136
- NATURE RESERVES AND PROTECTED AREAS IN LIPARI 136
  - Overview of Nature Reserves and Protected Areas 137
- TOP NATURE RESERVES AND PROTECTED AREAS IN LIPARI 138
  - Montagna della Guardia 138
  - Valle Muria 139
  - Punta del Perciato 139
  - Pumice Quarries 140
  - Activities in Lipari's Nature Reserves and Protected Areas
    141
  - Conservation Efforts and Environmental Responsibility .. 142

LIPARI'S CULINARY SCENE **143**

- DINING EXPERIENCES ON LIPARI 144
  - Wines and Beverages 146
  - Traditional Eolian Cuisine 147
  - Traditional Eolian Dishes 150
  - Eolian Beverages 151
- TOP RESTAURANTS AND EATERIES IN LIPARI 152
- Fine Dining and Upscale Restaurants *152*

COZY TRATTORIAS AND LOCAL FAVORITES 154
STREET FOOD AND CASUAL EATERIES 156
FOOD MARKETS AND STREET FOOD IN LIPARI 158
Street Food in Lipari... *159*
WINE TASTING AND LOCAL VINEYARDS IN LIPARI........................ 162
- The Winemaking Tradition in Lipari 162
- Local Wine Festivals and Events 165

CULTURE AND FESTIVALS IN LIPARI 167

FESTIVALS IN LIPARI 168
ANNUAL EVENTS AND FESTIVALS IN LIPARI................................. 171
1. Feast of San Bartolomeo (Festa di San Bartolomeo) *171*
2. Carnival of Lipari (Carnevale di Lipari) *172*
3. Aeolian Film Festival... *173*
4. Malvasia Wine Festival *174*
5. Festival of the Sea (Festa del Mare) *175*
6. Holy Week and Easter Celebrations (Settimana Santa e Pasqua)
.... *176*
LOCAL CUSTOMS AND TRADITIONS IN LIPARI: A GLIMPSE INTO
ISLAND LIFE 177
- Religious Devotion and Practices 177
- Family and Community Values 178
- Traditional Crafts and Artisanry.. 179
- Traditional Music and Dance 179
- Culinary Traditions 180
- Maritime Traditions... 180
- Celebrating Life Events... 181

SHOPPING OPTIONS.. 183

- Local Artisans and Handcrafted Goods.................................... 183
- Gourmet Food Products 184

SHOPPING DISTRICTS AND MARKETS 184
- Shopping Tips and Etiquette...185

SOUVENIRS AND LOCAL CRAFTS IN LIPARI.....................................185
- Handmade Ceramics: Art Inspired by Tradition 186
- Local Jewelry: Adornments with a Story...........................186
- Textiles and Embroidery: A Touch of Handmade Elegance 187
- Artistic Keepsakes: Paintings and Photography 187
- Aromatic Souvenirs: Perfumes and Soaps.........................188
- Supporting Local Artisans and Sustainable Shopping.......188

BEST SHOPPING STREETS AND MARKETS IN LIPARI: WHERE TO FIND THE PERFECT SOUVENIRS 189
- Corso Vittorio Emanuele 189
- Piazza di Marina Corta 190
- Via Garibaldi 191
- Lipari's Local Markets 192
- Specialty Stores and Hidden Gems................................193

ART GALLERIES AND BOUTIQUES IN LIPARI...................................194
- Galleria d'Arte Lipari 195
- Art Gallery Marina Corta..196

BOUTIQUES 196
- L'Arte della Ceramica 198

HIDDEN GEMS: UNIQUE FINDS AND LOCAL TREASURES...................199
- Mercato dell'Arte 199
- Bottega dei Fiori 200

DAY TRIPS AND EXCURSIONS: EXPLORING BEYOND LIPARI 201

VULCANO ISLAND 201
- Top Attractions on Vulcano Island..................................202
- Dining and Refreshments 204
- Practical Information..204

SALINA 205
- Top Attractions on Salina 206
- Experiencing Salina's Natural Beauty 208
- Cultural and Historical Sites 210
- Dining and Local Cuisine 210
- Practical Information 211

STROMBOLI 212
PANAREA 218
- Exploring Panarea's Natural Beauty 221

NIGHTLIFE AND ENTERTAINMENT IN LIPARI 227

BARS AND NIGHTCLUBS IN LIPARI 227
- Popular Bars 227
- Nightclubs 229

LIVE MUSIC VENUES AND SHOWS IN LIPARI 230
- Popular Live Music Venues 230
- Music Festivals and Events 232

EVENING ACTIVITIES IN LIPARI 233
- Sunset Cruises 233
- Stargazing 234
- Nighttime Walks 234
- Evening Markets and Street Fairs 235
- Outdoor Cinemas 235
- Dining Al Fresco 236

EXPLORING FAMILY-FRIENDLY LIPARI 237

BEACHES AND SWIMMING 237
OUTDOOR ADVENTURES 237
HISTORICAL AND CULTURAL EXPERIENCES 238
FAMILY-FRIENDLY DINING 239
PLAYGROUNDS AND PARKS 239

[x]

EVENTS AND FESTIVALS 240
KID-FRIENDLY ATTRACTIONS AND ACTIVITIES IN LIPARI 240
- Museo Archeologico Regionale Eoliano 240
- Lipari Castle 241
- Beaches and Water Activities 241
- Boat Tours 242
- Hiking and Nature Walks 242
- Playgrounds and Public Parks 243
- Local Events and Festivals 243
- Educational Tours 244

FAMILY ACCOMMODATION OPTIONS IN LIPARI 244
- Family-Friendly Hotels 244
- Apartments and Vacation Rentals 245
- Resorts with Family Amenities 246
- Budget-Friendly Options 246
- Camping and Outdoor Stays 247

WELLNESS AND RELAXATION IN LIPARI 255

SPAS AND WELLNESS CENTERS IN LIPARI 255
- Luxury Spas with Panoramic Views 255

WELLNESS CENTERS OFFERING HOLISTIC PROGRAMS 256
NATURAL HOT SPRINGS AND THERMAL BATHS 257
WELLNESS RETREATS AND YOGA CENTERS 258
RELAXING BEACHES AND SECLUDED COVES IN LIPARI 259
- Spiaggia di Canneto 259
- Spiaggia Bianca 260
- Acquacalda Beach 261

SECLUDED COVES: HIDDEN GEMS FOR SOLITUDE SEEKERS 261
- Porticello 262
- Coral Beach 263

xi | Page

PRACTICAL INFORMATION FOR VISITING LIPARI....265

- Language and Communication 265
- Currency and Payments 265
- Time Zone 265
- Electricity and Plug Type 266
- Emergency Contacts 266
- Internet and Connectivity 266
- Local Etiquette 266
- Health and Safety Precautions 267
- Transportation on the Island 267
- Climate Considerations 267
- Local Customs and Traditions 267
- Tipping Guidelines 268

LANGUAGE TIPS AND COMMON PHRASES 268
- Additional Tips 270

USEFUL WEBSITES AND RESOURCES *270*

ITINERARIES AND SUGGESTED ROUTES FOR EXPLORING LIPARI 273

1-DAY ITINERARY: HIGHLIGHTS OF LIPARI 273
- Morning: Dive into History and Culture 273
- Midday: Savor Local Flavors 274
- Afternoon: Relax and Enjoy the Scenery 274
- Evening: Enjoy a Seaside Dinner 275
- Late Evening: Stroll Along the Waterfront 276

3-DAY ITINERARY: A DEEPER EXPLORATION OF LIPARI 276
- Day 1: Historical and Cultural Immersion 276
- Day 2: Island Exploration and Coastal Adventures 278
- Day 3: Cultural Immersion and Local Flavors 279

7-DAY ITINERARY: THE ULTIMATE LIPARI EXPERIENCE 281
- Day 1: Arrival and Initial Exploration 281
- Day 2: Dive into History and Culture 282

- Day 3: Island Adventures and Coastal Beauty 283
- Day 4: Nature and Outdoor Activities 284
- Day 5: Cultural Insights and Relaxation 285
- Day 6: Water Activities and Island Exploration 286
- Day 7: Final Day of Exploration and Reflection 287

SPECIAL INTEREST ITINERARIES: TAILORED EXPERIENCES IN LIPARI 288

- History and Culture Itinerary 288
- Nature and Adventure Itinerary 289
- Culinary Exploration Itinerary 290
- Art and Craft Itinerary 292
- Wellness and Relaxation Itinerary 293

CONCLUSION 295

MY JOURNAL 297

ALLOW YOUR IMAGINATION TO CRAFT THE SCENES AS YOU TRAVERSE THROUGH DIVERSE AND CAPTIVATING LANDSCAPES DIFFERENT FROM YOUR EVERYDAY HORIZON.

Michael Z. Wilson

WELCOME TO LIPARI

Lipari, the largest and liveliest of the Aeolian Islands, is a captivating blend of natural beauty and cultural richness. With its volcanic landscapes, clear blue waters, and charming towns, Lipari is a destination that enchants visitors from the moment they arrive. The island's unique geography, shaped by ancient volcanic activity, has given rise to stunning cliffs, serene beaches, and panoramic views that are simply breathtaking.

Overview of Lipari

Lipari is a volcanic archipelago located off the northern coast of Sicily in the Tyrrhenian Sea. Often referred to as the heart of the Aeolian Islands, Lipari serves as the central hub for travelers exploring this UNESCO World Heritage-listed region. The island's strategic position, combined with its natural beauty and cultural wealth, makes it a prime destination for those seeking both adventure and relaxation.

The island's landscape is a testament to its volcanic origins, with rugged terrain, dramatic cliffs, and a coastline that alternates between sandy beaches and rocky shores. Volcanic activity has given Lipari its distinctive black and white pumice stone cliffs, which contrast strikingly with the deep blue of the surrounding sea. The island's highest point, Monte Chirica, offers panoramic views that stretch across the entire archipelago, providing a breathtaking perspective on Lipari's unique geography.

A Vibrant Island Life

Lipari is a lively and bustling island, particularly during the summer months when tourists from around the world flock to its shores. Lipari Town, the island's main settlement, is a charming blend of narrow streets, colorful houses, and historic buildings. The town is centered around the Marina Corta, a picturesque harbor filled with fishing boats and lined with cafes, restaurants, and shops. Here, visitors can enjoy the relaxed island atmosphere, sampling local delicacies, shopping for handmade crafts, or simply watching the world go by.

Natural Wonders and Outdoor Adventures

For nature lovers and outdoor enthusiasts, Lipari offers a wealth of activities. The island's rugged terrain is crisscrossed by hiking trails that lead to secluded coves, ancient ruins, and panoramic viewpoints. The coastal areas are ideal for water sports, with opportunities for swimming, snorkeling, diving, and kayaking. Boat tours around the island provide a unique perspective on Lipari's coastline, revealing hidden caves, grottos, and secluded beaches that are otherwise inaccessible.

A Culinary Delight

Lipari's culinary scene is a highlight for many visitors, offering a taste of traditional Aeolian cuisine, which is heavily influenced by the island's maritime heritage. Fresh seafood is a staple, with dishes featuring locally caught fish, octopus, and shellfish. The island's fertile soil also produces a variety of fruits, vegetables, and herbs, which are used in local dishes like caponata (a sweet and sour vegetable stew) and pasta alla Liparota (pasta with tomatoes, capers, and olives). The local Malvasia wine, a sweet dessert wine made from grapes grown on the island, is a must-try for any visitor.

A Gateway to the Aeolian Islands

Lipari's central location makes it the ideal base for exploring the other Aeolian Islands, each of which has its own unique character and attractions. Regular ferry services connect Lipari to the neighboring islands of Vulcano, Salina, Stromboli, Panarea, Filicudi, and Alicudi, allowing visitors to easily hop between them. Whether you're interested in hiking up an active volcano, relaxing on a black sand beach, or exploring ancient ruins, Lipari offers easy access to all the wonders of the Aeolian archipelago.

A Year-Round Destination

While Lipari is most popular during the summer months, the island is a year-round destination, with each season offering a different experience. Spring and autumn are ideal for those who prefer milder weather and fewer crowds, while winter provides a peaceful retreat, with many of the island's residents returning to their traditional ways of life. No matter when you visit, Lipari's natural beauty, rich history, and warm hospitality ensure an unforgettable experience.

Brief History and Cultural Significance of Lipari

The history of Lipari dates back to the dawn of human civilization, with archaeological findings suggesting that the island has been inhabited since the Neolithic period, around 4000 BC. Early settlers were attracted by the island's rich resources, particularly obsidian, a volcanic glass used to make tools and weapons. Lipari became a major center for obsidian trade, with its sharp-edged tools spreading across the Mediterranean. This early industry laid the foundation for Lipari's long-standing role as a crossroads of cultures and commerce.

The Greek Era: Aeolian Influence

Around the 6th century BC, Lipari became a Greek colony, part of the broader Hellenic world. The island was named after Aeolus, the god of winds, who, according to mythology, resided in the Aeolian Islands. The Greeks fortified Lipari with strong walls and developed it into a prosperous city-state. During this period, Lipari became known for its flourishing economy, vibrant culture, and strategic naval power. The influence of Greek culture is still evident in Lipari's architecture, language, and religious practices, with remnants of ancient Greek temples and pottery found throughout the island.

Roman Conquest: A Time of Transition

Lipari's prominence continued into the Roman era after the island was conquered by the Romans in 252 BC during the First Punic War. Under Roman rule, Lipari became an important naval base and a center for agriculture and fishing. The island's strategic location made it a key point in the Mediterranean trade routes, and its residents enjoyed relative peace and prosperity. Roman influence is visible in the ruins of ancient villas, aqueducts, and thermal baths that dot the island, offering a glimpse into the life of Lipari's inhabitants during this period.

Byzantine and Medieval Times: A Fortress of Faith

Following the fall of the Western Roman Empire, Lipari came under Byzantine control, which introduced Christianity to the island. The construction of churches and monasteries became prominent, and Lipari was often attacked by pirates and invaders due to its strategic location. During the early Middle Ages, the island was fortified to protect its inhabitants from these threats. The construction of the Lipari Castle, perched on a volcanic rock overlooking the town, began during this time and continued to expand over the centuries. This fortress became a symbol of the island's resilience and played a crucial role in defending Lipari from Saracen raids and other invasions.

Norman and Spanish Rule: A Cultural Melting Pot

In the 11th century, Lipari came under Norman control, which brought a period of stability and growth. The Normans rebuilt and expanded the island's fortifications and churches, leaving a lasting architectural legacy. The island later became part of the Kingdom of Sicily and experienced a period of Spanish rule during the 16th and 17th centuries. Under Spanish influence, Lipari's culture became a unique blend of Norman, Byzantine, and Spanish elements. The Cathedral of San Bartolomeo, the island's patron saint, was built during this time and remains one of Lipari's most significant religious sites.

The Modern Era: Cultural Revival and Tourism

Lipari's fortunes declined in the 18th and 19th centuries, with many residents emigrating due to economic hardships and natural disasters, including volcanic eruptions and earthquakes. However, the 20th century brought a revival, with the island gradually developing into a popular tourist destination. The preservation of Lipari's historical sites and cultural heritage became a priority, and today, the island is celebrated for its rich history, which is meticulously showcased in the Museo Archeologico Regionale Eoliano. This museum, located within the Lipari Castle complex, houses an extensive collection of artifacts from the island's long history, including prehistoric tools, Greek ceramics, and Roman sculptures.

Cultural Significance

Lipari's cultural significance is deeply rooted in its diverse history, with each era leaving its mark on the island's traditions, architecture, and way of life. The island's festivals and religious celebrations are a vibrant expression of this cultural heritage. The Festa di San Bartolomeo, held every August, is the most important festival on the island, celebrating the patron saint of Lipari with processions, fireworks, and communal feasts. This festival, along with other local customs, reflects the islanders' deep connection to their history and faith.

Lipari's cultural landscape is also enriched by its maritime heritage. Fishing has been a way of life for generations, and the island's cuisine is a testament to this, with dishes featuring locally caught seafood and traditional Aeolian flavors. The local dialect, a blend of Italian, Sicilian, and remnants of ancient languages, further highlights Lipari's unique cultural identity.

A Living Legacy

Today, Lipari stands as a living testament to the many cultures and civilizations that have shaped it over millennia. The island's rich history is not just preserved in its museums and ancient ruins but is also alive in the daily lives of its residents, in their customs, language, and celebrations. For visitors, Lipari offers a unique opportunity to experience a place where history and culture are woven into the very fabric of everyday life, making it a destination that is both historically significant and culturally enriching.

Climate and Best Time to Visit Lipari

Lipari enjoys a classic Mediterranean climate, characterized by warm, dry summers and mild, wet winters. This type of climate makes the island a pleasant destination throughout most of the year, with each season offering its own unique charm.

- **Summer (June to August):** Summers in Lipari are typically hot and sunny, with average daytime temperatures ranging from 28°C to 32°C (82°F to 90°F). The heat is tempered by refreshing sea breezes, especially along the coast. This is the peak tourist season, with July and August being the busiest months as travelers flock to Lipari for its beaches, outdoor activities, and festivals. The warm sea temperatures, averaging around 25°C (77°F), make it an ideal time for swimming, snorkeling, and other water sports. The long daylight hours provide plenty of time to explore the island's attractions and natural beauty.

- **Autumn (September to November):** Autumn in Lipari is a season of transition, with temperatures gradually cooling down from the summer heat. September remains warm, with temperatures around 25°C to 28°C (77°F to 82°F), making it a great time to visit if you prefer fewer crowds and a more relaxed atmosphere. By October, temperatures range between 20°C to 24°C (68°F to 75°F), and the island's landscape begins to take on the rich colors of fall. This period is ideal for hiking, exploring the island's archaeological sites, and enjoying the grape harvest season, which is celebrated with local wine festivals. Rain showers become more frequent in November, but they are usually short-lived, leaving plenty of time to enjoy outdoor activities.
- **Winter (December to February):** Winters in Lipari are mild, with temperatures typically ranging from 10°C to 15°C (50°F to 59°F). While this is the off-season for tourism, the island retains a quiet, peaceful charm that appeals to those looking for a tranquil retreat. Rainfall is more common during these months, especially in December and January, but there are still plenty of sunny days. The winter season offers an opportunity to experience Lipari's authentic local culture, as the island's residents go

about their daily lives away from the tourist crowds. It's also a great time to explore the island's museums, enjoy the local cuisine, and take part in the traditional Christmas and New Year celebrations.
- **Spring (March to May):** Spring is a particularly beautiful time to visit Lipari, as the island bursts into bloom with wildflowers and lush vegetation. Temperatures during this season range from 15°C to 22°C (59°F to 72°F), providing a comfortable climate for outdoor activities. April and May are especially pleasant, with longer days and minimal rainfall. This is an excellent time for hiking, cycling, and exploring the island's natural beauty without the heat of summer. The spring months also see the start of the tourist season, but the island remains relatively uncrowded, offering a more serene experience for visitors.

The Best Time to Visit Lipari

While Lipari is a year-round destination, the best time to visit depends on your preferences and the type of experience you're seeking:

- **For Beach Lovers and Water Activities:** If your primary goal is to enjoy Lipari's stunning beaches and crystal-clear waters, the best time to visit is during the summer months (June to August). The warm sea temperatures and consistent sunshine make it perfect for swimming, snorkeling, and sunbathing. However, be prepared for larger crowds, especially in July and August.
- **For Outdoor Enthusiasts and Hikers:** Spring (March to May) and early autumn (September to October) are the best times for hiking, cycling, and exploring Lipari's natural

landscapes. The weather is mild, and the island's flora is at its most vibrant, offering breathtaking views and a more tranquil atmosphere. These months are also ideal for those looking to explore the island's cultural and historical sites without the summer heat.
- **For Cultural Experiences and Local Festivals:** Visiting in late summer or early autumn allows you to experience Lipari's rich cultural traditions, including the Festa di San Bartolomeo in August, which is the island's most significant religious festival. Autumn also brings wine harvest celebrations and other local events that offer a glimpse into the island's way of life.
- **For a Quiet, Relaxing Getaway:** If you prefer a quieter, more reflective experience, consider visiting during the winter months (December to February). While the weather is cooler and some tourist facilities may be closed, the peaceful ambiance and authentic local culture make it a rewarding time to visit. Winter is also the best time to find lower accommodation rates and enjoy the island's attractions without the crowds.

Weather Considerations and Tips

- **Sun Protection:** No matter when you visit, it's essential to protect yourself from the sun, especially during the summer months. Sunscreen, hats, and sunglasses are a must, and it's advisable to stay hydrated and seek shade during the hottest part of the day.
- **Layered Clothing:** In spring and autumn, the weather can be unpredictable, with cooler mornings and evenings. Packing layered clothing will help you stay comfortable throughout the day.

- **Rain Gear:** If visiting in winter or late autumn, be prepared for occasional rain showers by packing a light raincoat or umbrella.
- **Advanced Bookings:** During the peak summer season, it's advisable to book accommodation and ferry tickets well in advance, as the island can get fully booked.

In summary, Lipari's climate makes it an attractive destination throughout the year, with each season offering distinct experiences. It doesn't matter if you're drawn to its sun-soaked beaches, scenic hiking trails, or rich cultural heritage, Lipari has something to offer every traveler, no matter when you choose to visit

HOW TO GET TO LIPARI

Getting to Lipari is an adventure in itself, as the island is only accessible by sea. If you're coming from mainland Italy, Sicily, or another Aeolian Island, there are several convenient options for reaching Lipari. Most travelers begin their journey by flying or taking a train to one of the nearby cities, followed by a ferry or hydrofoil ride to the island.

By Air

The closest airports to Lipari are located on the island of Sicily. From these airports, you can easily reach the ports that offer ferry and hydrofoil services to Lipari.

- **Catania Fontanarossa Airport (CTA):** Located about 150 kilometers (93 miles) from the port of Milazzo, Catania Fontanarossa Airport is the largest and busiest airport in Sicily. It offers numerous international and domestic flights, making it the most popular choice for travelers heading to Lipari. Upon arrival, you can take a bus or private transfer from the airport to Milazzo, where you can catch a ferry or hydrofoil to Lipari.
- **Palermo Falcone-Borsellino Airport (PMO):** Situated approximately 225 kilometers (140 miles) from Milazzo, Palermo's airport is another option for travelers. While slightly farther from the main departure port, Palermo offers connections to several other Sicilian ports that provide ferry services to Lipari, such as Cefalù and Messina.
- **Reggio Calabria Airport (REG):** Located on the mainland, Reggio Calabria Airport is a smaller airport but

offers another gateway to the Aeolian Islands. From Reggio Calabria, you can take a ferry directly to Lipari during the summer season, though this option is less frequent.

By Train

If you prefer to travel by train, several rail routes connect mainland Italy and Sicily to the ports that offer ferry services to Lipari. Trains are a comfortable and scenic way to reach the embarkation points.

- **From Rome or Naples:** You can take a train from Rome or Naples to Milazzo, Messina, or Palermo, depending on your port of departure. The journey from Rome to Milazzo typically takes about 9 to 10 hours, while the trip from Naples is slightly shorter. Trains from these cities often include an overnight option, allowing you to rest before your ferry journey.
- **From Catania or Palermo:** Regional trains connect Catania and Palermo to the ports of Milazzo, Messina, and Cefalù. The train ride from Catania to Milazzo takes approximately 2 hours, while the trip from Palermo to Milazzo is around 3 hours.
- **From Reggio Calabria:** Reggio Calabria is well connected to various parts of Italy by train. After arriving at the Reggio Calabria train station, you can head to the port for a ferry to Lipari.

By Ferry or Hydrofoil

Once you've reached your chosen port, the final step is to take a ferry or hydrofoil to Lipari. The port of Milazzo is the most common departure point, but you can also catch ferries from

Messina, Naples, Palermo, and other locations. Here's a breakdown of the options:

- **From Milazzo:** Milazzo is the primary gateway to the Aeolian Islands, including Lipari. The port is located on the northeastern coast of Sicily, and it's the closest departure point to Lipari. Ferries and hydrofoils operated by companies like Liberty Lines and Siremar run frequent services throughout the day. The journey from Milazzo to Lipari typically takes between 1 and 2 hours, depending on the vessel type. Hydrofoils are faster, taking about 1 hour, while ferries offer a more leisurely 2-hour crossing.
- **From Messina:** Messina, located further south on Sicily's eastern coast, also offers ferry services to Lipari. The journey from Messina takes about 1.5 to 2.5 hours, depending on the ferry operator and the number of stops along the way. Messina is well-connected by train and bus, making it a convenient alternative for travelers who prefer to avoid Milazzo.
- **From Naples:** Naples offers ferry services to Lipari during the summer months. The overnight ferry journey takes approximately 12 to 14 hours, making it a good option for travelers who want to combine transportation with a night of rest. SNAV and Alilauro are the primary operators for this route. This longer journey can be a relaxing way to arrive at Lipari, with the added bonus of waking up to views of the Aeolian Islands as you approach.
- **From Palermo and Cefalù:** Palermo and Cefalù offer seasonal ferry services to Lipari, typically during the summer months. These ferries take around 4 to 5 hours, providing a scenic journey along the northern coast of Sicily before heading to the Aeolian Islands. Palermo is

particularly convenient for those flying into the city or exploring other parts of western Sicily before heading to Lipari.
- **From Reggio Calabria:** During the summer season, Reggio Calabria on the Italian mainland offers ferry services to Lipari. This route takes approximately 2 hours and is operated by Liberty Lines. While less frequent than the Sicilian routes, it provides a direct link for travelers coming from Calabria or other parts of mainland Italy.

By Private Boat or Yacht

For those seeking a more personalized experience, chartering a private boat or yacht is an option. Several companies offer yacht rentals and private boat transfers from various ports in Sicily and southern Italy. This option provides flexibility in terms of departure times and allows you to tailor your journey to Lipari according to your preferences. Additionally, a private boat offers the opportunity to explore hidden coves and beaches around Lipari and the other Aeolian Islands at your own pace.

Practical Tips for Your Journey

- **Advance Booking:** During the peak tourist season (June to September), it's advisable to book your ferry or hydrofoil tickets in advance, as services can fill up quickly. Online booking is available for most ferry operators.
- **Port Transfers:** If you're arriving at one of Sicily's airports, several transfer services and buses are available to take you directly to the port of Milazzo or other departure points. These transfers can be booked in advance or arranged upon arrival.

- **Luggage:** Most ferries and hydrofoils have luggage storage areas, but space can be limited, especially during busy times. Pack light if possible, and be prepared to carry your bags on and off the vessels.
- **Timing:** Consider the time of day when planning your journey to Lipari. Early morning and late afternoon ferries are popular, but mid-day departures are often less crowded. If you're traveling during the summer, keep in mind that ferry services can be affected by weather conditions, so it's wise to allow some flexibility in your schedule.
- **Accommodation Near Ports:** If you have an early morning ferry, consider staying overnight in Milazzo, Messina, or another port city to ensure a stress-free departure. There are numerous hotels and guesthouses near the ports.

In conclusion, getting to Lipari involves a combination of air, rail, and sea travel, offering a variety of routes and experiences. Whether you choose the fastest hydrofoil, a scenic ferry ride, or a private boat, the journey to Lipari is part of the adventure, setting the stage for your exploration of this enchanting Aeolian island.

GETTING READY FOR YOUR TRIP TO LIPARI

Preparing for a trip to Lipari requires thoughtful planning to ensure a smooth and enjoyable experience. From booking transportation and accommodations to packing the right essentials, taking care of these details in advance will help you make the most of your time on the island.

Booking Travel and Accommodation
- **Travel Arrangements:** Since Lipari is an island, your journey will involve multiple modes of transportation, including flights, trains, and ferries. It's crucial to book these well in advance, especially during the busy summer months. If you're flying into Sicily or taking a train from another part of Italy, coordinating your arrival time with the ferry schedule is key to avoiding long waits at the port. Online booking options make it easier to secure your tickets and ensure a hassle-free trip.
- **Accommodation:** Lipari offers a range of lodging options, from luxury hotels to charming bed-and-breakfasts. Since the island is a popular destination, especially in the summer, it's wise to reserve your accommodation early. Consider the location of your stay—whether you prefer being close to the town center for easy access to restaurants and shops, or you'd rather be near the beach for quick dips in the sea.

Planning Activities and Itineraries

- **Research and Reservations:** While spontaneous exploration is part of the charm of visiting Lipari, it's helpful to research and plan key activities in advance. This includes booking guided tours, boat trips, or entry to popular attractions, which can fill up quickly during peak seasons.
- **Itinerary Flexibility:** Plan your itinerary with some flexibility to accommodate changes in weather or ferry schedules. Having a mix of activities, such as sightseeing, beach time, and cultural experiences, will help you enjoy the island's diversity.

Understanding Local Customs and Language

- **Language Preparation:** While Italian is the official language, English is commonly spoken in tourist areas. However, learning a few basic Italian phrases can enhance your experience and show respect for the local culture.
- **Cultural Awareness:** Familiarize yourself with local customs, such as greeting people with a friendly "Buongiorno" (Good morning) or "Buonasera" (Good evening). Understanding dining etiquette and tipping practices will also help you navigate social situations more comfortably.

Health and Safety Considerations

- **Travel Insurance:** Consider purchasing travel insurance that covers medical emergencies, trip cancellations, and other unexpected events. This provides peace of mind, especially when traveling to a remote island.

- **Health Precautions:** If you have any specific health needs, ensure you have enough medication for the duration of your trip, as pharmacies on the island might not carry everything you need. It's also wise to check the latest health and travel advisories before your departure.

Currency and Budgeting

- **Currency:** The official currency in Lipari, like the rest of Italy, is the Euro (€). While credit cards are widely accepted, it's a good idea to carry some cash for small purchases, especially in more remote areas of the island.
- **Budget Planning:** Plan your budget by considering costs for accommodation, meals, activities, and transportation. Prices can vary depending on the season, with summer being more expensive due to higher demand. It's helpful to set aside some extra funds for spontaneous purchases or unexpected expenses.

Final Checklist: Ready to Go

As your departure date approaches, double-check your reservations, pack your bags, and make sure all your travel documents are in order. Preparing thoroughly will allow you to relax and fully immerse yourself in the beauty and culture of Lipari once you arrive.

With these preparations in place, you'll be well-equipped to enjoy a memorable and stress-free trip to Lipari, ready to explore its natural wonders, rich history, and vibrant local life.

Travel Documents and Visa Requirements for Lipari

Before embarking on your journey to Lipari, ensuring you have the correct travel documents and understanding visa requirements is crucial. Being prepared in advance can save you time and potential complications upon arrival. Here's a detailed guide to what you need to know.

Passports and Identification

- **Passport Requirements:** If you're traveling to Lipari from outside of Italy, a valid passport is essential for entry into the country. Your passport should be valid for at least six months beyond your planned departure date from Italy. This is a standard requirement for most international travelers and helps avoid any issues at immigration.
- **EU/EEA Citizens:** Citizens of the European Union (EU) and the European Economic Area (EEA) do not need a passport to enter Italy. A valid national identity card is sufficient for travel within these regions. However, carrying a passport may still be advisable for identification purposes during your stay.
- **Children and Minors:** If you're traveling with children, they will also need their own passport or identity card, depending on their nationality. Ensure that all documents are up-to-date and that any necessary permissions for traveling with minors are in place, especially if only one parent is accompanying the child.

Visa Requirements

- **Schengen Area Visa:** Italy is part of the Schengen Area, a group of 27 European countries that have abolished passport control at their mutual borders. This means that travelers from other Schengen countries can enter Italy without needing a visa. If you are from a non-Schengen country, you'll need to determine if a visa is required for entry into Italy.
- **Visa-Exempt Countries:** Citizens of several countries, including the United States, Canada, Australia, New Zealand, and Japan, can enter Italy for short stays (up to 90 days within a 180-day period) without a visa, as long as the purpose of the visit is tourism, business, or family visits. This exemption applies to the entire Schengen Area, meaning you can travel freely within the member countries during this period.
- **Countries Requiring a Visa:** If you are from a country that requires a visa to enter the Schengen Area, you'll need to apply for a Schengen Visa before your trip. The application process usually involves providing a valid passport, recent passport-sized photos, proof of travel insurance, accommodation details, and a travel itinerary. You may also need to show proof of sufficient funds for your stay and a return ticket.
- **Longer Stays and Special Visas:** If you plan to stay in Italy for more than 90 days or for purposes other than tourism (such as work or study), you will need to apply for a different type of visa. Long-term visas require additional documentation and often involve a more complex application process. It's important to apply well in advance of your travel dates, as processing times can vary.

Travel Insurance

- **Health Insurance Requirements:** While not always mandatory, having travel health insurance that covers medical emergencies and repatriation is highly recommended. If you need to apply for a Schengen Visa, proof of travel insurance with the required coverage amount is required. This insurance should be valid throughout your stay in the Schengen Area.
- **Trip Cancellation and Interruption Insurance:** Consider purchasing additional travel insurance that covers trip cancellations, delays, or interruptions, as well as lost or stolen luggage. This can provide peace of mind and financial protection against unforeseen circumstances that could disrupt your travel plans.

Customs and Entry Procedures

- **Arrival in Italy:** Upon arriving in Italy, you'll go through customs and passport control. If you're entering from another Schengen country, passport control may not be required. However, if you're arriving from a non-Schengen country, you will need to present your passport and, if applicable, your visa. Be prepared to answer basic questions about the purpose of your visit and your travel plans.
- **Customs Declarations:** If you're carrying items that exceed the duty-free allowance, such as alcohol, tobacco, or high-value goods, you may need to declare them at customs. Italy has specific regulations regarding the importation of certain goods, including food, plants, and animals, so it's advisable to check these rules before you travel.

Important Considerations

- **ETIAS Authorization (Starting 2024):** Beginning in 2024, travelers from visa-exempt countries will need to apply for an ETIAS (European Travel Information and Authorization System) authorization before entering the Schengen Area. This is not a visa, but rather an electronic travel authorization that will be required for short-term stays. The ETIAS application will involve a background check and a small fee, and it must be completed online before your trip.
- **Renewal and Expiration of Documents:** Ensure that your passport and any necessary visas or travel authorizations are valid and up-to-date before your trip. Renew any documents that are close to expiring well in advance to avoid any last-minute issues.
- **Emergency Contacts:** It's wise to keep a copy of your passport, visa, and travel insurance documents in a safe place, separate from the originals. Additionally, note down the contact information for your country's embassy or consulate in Italy, as well as any emergency contact numbers you might need during your trip.

Final Preparations

As you finalize your preparations for Lipari, double-check all travel documents, visa requirements, and insurance policies to ensure they meet Italian entry requirements. Having everything in order will allow you to focus on enjoying your journey to this beautiful island without any unnecessary stress or complications.

By taking these steps, you can ensure a smooth entry into Italy and a trouble-free stay on Lipari, leaving you free to explore the island's stunning landscapes and rich cultural heritage.

Currency, Banking, and Budgeting Tips for Lipari

Currency Overview

- **Official Currency:** The official currency in Lipari, as in the rest of Italy, is the Euro (€). The Euro is used throughout most European Union countries, making it convenient if you're traveling to other parts of Europe before or after your visit to Lipari.
- **Currency Denominations:** Euro banknotes are available in denominations of €5, €10, €20, €50, €100, €200, and €500, though the higher denominations may not be widely accepted for smaller purchases. Coins come in values of 1, 2, 5, 10, 20, and 50 cents, as well as €1 and €2.

Banking Services on Lipari

- **ATMs (Bancomat):** Lipari has several ATMs (known locally as "Bancomat") located throughout the main town and in some of the smaller villages. These machines are typically connected to international networks, allowing you to withdraw Euros directly using your debit or credit card. Be aware that ATMs in more remote areas of the island might occasionally run out of cash, especially during peak tourist seasons, so it's wise to withdraw enough money in advance.
- **Bank Opening Hours:** Banks on Lipari generally operate from Monday to Friday, with hours typically from 8:30 a.m. to 1:30 p.m., and then reopening for a shorter period in the afternoon from 2:45 p.m. to 3:45 p.m. Most banks are closed on weekends and public holidays. It's important to plan your banking needs around these hours, especially if

you need to exchange currency or conduct other banking transactions.
- **Currency Exchange:** Currency exchange services are available at some banks, though the rates may not be as favorable as those found at ATMs. If you prefer to exchange money rather than withdraw it from an ATM, do so at a bank or a reputable currency exchange office. It's advisable to avoid exchanging money at airports or hotels, as these locations often charge higher fees and offer less favorable rates.
- **Credit and Debit Cards:** Credit and debit cards are widely accepted on Lipari, particularly Visa and Mastercard. American Express and Diners Club cards may not be as commonly accepted, especially in smaller establishments. When using a card, always check if there are any additional fees for foreign transactions, as some banks charge a small percentage for international purchases.
- **Traveler's Checks:** Traveler's checks are becoming increasingly uncommon and may be difficult to cash in Lipari. If you do choose to bring them, ensure they are in Euros to avoid additional exchange fees. However, due to the convenience and security of credit cards and ATMs, traveler's checks are not generally recommended for this destination.

Budgeting Tips for Your Trip to Lipari

- **Accommodation Costs:** Accommodation in Lipari varies widely depending on the time of year, location, and type of lodging. During the peak summer months (July and August), prices can be significantly higher, especially for hotels and luxury accommodations. To save money, consider visiting in the shoulder seasons (April to June or September to October), when prices are lower and the weather is still pleasant. Budget options such as guesthouses, B&Bs, and vacation rentals are also available, offering more affordable alternatives to hotels.

- **Dining and Food Costs:** Dining out in Lipari can range from budget-friendly meals at casual eateries to more expensive options at fine dining restaurants. A typical meal at a mid-range restaurant might cost between €15 and €30 per person, while budget travelers can find pizzas, paninis, or snacks for under €10. For an authentic and cost-effective experience, consider shopping at local markets and preparing some meals yourself if your accommodation has a kitchen. Sampling street food, like arancini (stuffed rice balls) or cannoli (sweet pastry rolls), is another way to enjoy local flavors without overspending.
- **Transportation Expenses:** The primary costs for transportation to and around Lipari include ferry tickets, local bus fares, and possibly car or scooter rentals. Ferries from mainland Italy or Sicily to Lipari can vary in price depending on the season and the type of service (regular or hydrofoil). Local bus services on the island are inexpensive, but schedules may be limited, especially in off-peak seasons. Renting a scooter or small car is a convenient way to explore the island, with daily rental rates starting at around €30 to €50. If you plan to rent a vehicle, factor in the cost of fuel, which can be higher on the islands than on the mainland.
- **Sightseeing and Activities:** Many of Lipari's attractions, such as its beautiful beaches, historic sites, and hiking trails, are free or low-cost. However, guided tours, museum

entries, and boat excursions can add to your budget. Museum entrance fees typically range from €5 to €10, while a full-day boat tour around the Aeolian Islands might cost between €40 and €70 per person. Consider prioritizing activities that interest you most and look for package deals that combine several experiences at a discounted rate.

- **Shopping and Souvenirs:** Lipari is known for its local crafts, including pottery, jewelry, and food products like capers and Malvasia wine. Prices for souvenirs can vary, so it's a good idea to shop around before making a purchase. Local markets and small shops often offer unique items at reasonable prices. If you're on a tight budget, set a limit on souvenir spending and focus on smaller, meaningful items that won't break the bank.

Money-Saving Tips

- **Avoid Dynamic Currency Conversion:** When paying by card, you might be offered the choice of being charged in your home currency instead of Euros. This is known as Dynamic Currency Conversion (DCC). While it might seem convenient, DCC usually comes with higher fees and an unfavorable exchange rate. Always choose to pay in Euros to get a better deal.
- **Use ATMs Wisely:** If you need to withdraw cash, use ATMs attached to reputable banks, as they tend to offer the best exchange rates and lowest fees. Avoid standalone ATMs, which may charge higher fees. Also, consider withdrawing larger amounts at once to minimize transaction fees.
- **Consider a Multi-Currency Card:** If you're planning to visit multiple countries or want to minimize currency

conversion fees, consider using a multi-currency travel card. These cards allow you to load different currencies onto the card, locking in exchange rates in advance and reducing the need for multiple conversions.
- **Prepaid Travel Cards:** Prepaid travel cards can be a safe and convenient way to manage your travel budget. You can load a specific amount onto the card in Euros and use it like a debit card. These cards often come with lower fees than credit cards for foreign transactions and can help you stick to your budget by limiting overspending.
- **Track Your Spending:** Keeping track of your expenses during your trip can help you stay within your budget. Use a travel budgeting app or simply keep a daily record of what you're spending. This can help you identify areas where you might need to cut back and ensure you don't run out of funds before the end of your trip.
- **Save on Dining:** To save on dining costs, consider having your main meal at lunchtime, when many restaurants offer set menus at a lower price than the evening à la carte options. Additionally, explore local trattorias and pizzerias, which often provide excellent food at more affordable prices than tourist-oriented restaurants.

By following these currency, banking, and budgeting tips, you can manage your finances effectively while enjoying all that Lipari has to offer. With careful planning and smart spending, you can make the most of your trip without breaking the bank, ensuring a memorable and stress-free experience on this beautiful island.

Packing Guide: What to Bring to Lipari

Clothing Essentials

- **Lightweight Layers:** Lipari's Mediterranean climate means warm summers and mild winters. Packing lightweight, breathable clothing is key. Cotton, linen, and moisture-wicking fabrics will keep you comfortable during the hot summer months. Bring a mix of T-shirts, tank tops, and lightweight long-sleeve shirts for sun protection.
- **Evening Wear:** While the island has a relaxed vibe, dining out at certain restaurants may require slightly dressier attire. Consider bringing a smart-casual outfit such as a sundress, nice blouse with trousers, or a collared shirt with chinos. A light jacket or shawl is also useful for cooler evenings, especially if you're visiting during the shoulder seasons of spring or fall.
- **Swimwear:** Swimwear is a must for Lipari's beautiful beaches and crystal-clear waters. Bring at least two swimsuits so you always have a dry one ready. A cover-up or sarong is also handy for transitioning from beach to town or for lounging by the pool.
- **Footwear:** Comfortable walking shoes or sandals are essential for exploring the island's cobblestone streets and hiking trails. If you plan on hiking, bring sturdy shoes with good grip. Flip-flops or water shoes are ideal for the beach, as some of Lipari's shores are rocky rather than sandy.
- **Rain Gear:** Although Lipari enjoys sunny weather most of the year, the occasional rain shower is possible, especially in the winter. A lightweight, packable rain jacket or poncho will keep you dry without taking up much space in your luggage.

- **Sun Protection:** The Mediterranean sun can be intense, so pack a wide-brimmed hat, sunglasses with UV protection, and plenty of sunscreen. A high-SPF, water-resistant sunscreen is recommended, especially if you plan on spending a lot of time at the beach or on the water.

Beach and Water Gear

- **Snorkeling Equipment:** If you enjoy snorkeling, consider bringing your own mask, snorkel, and fins. While you can rent equipment on the island, having your own ensures a better fit and comfort. Lipari's clear waters are perfect for underwater exploration, so this is a must for ocean enthusiasts.
- **Towels and Beach Mat:** Many hotels provide towels, but it's a good idea to bring a quick-dry travel towel for the beach. A lightweight beach mat or a large sarong can also be useful for lounging on the sand.
- **Reusable Water Bottle:** Staying hydrated is essential, especially in the hot summer months. A reusable water bottle with a built-in filter can help you stay refreshed and reduce plastic waste. Many accommodations and restaurants are happy to refill water bottles for you.

Electronics and Travel Gadgets

- **Adapters and Chargers:** Italy uses Type C, F, and L plugs with a standard voltage of 230V. If your electronics are not compatible, bring a universal travel adapter. Don't forget chargers for your phone, camera, and other devices, and consider a portable power bank for days when you're out exploring all day.

- **Camera:** Lipari's stunning landscapes and historic sites make for fantastic photo opportunities. Whether you're a smartphone photographer or prefer a DSLR, make sure your camera is ready to capture the beauty of the island. Bring extra memory cards and batteries to avoid missing out on any shots.
- **Travel Apps and Maps:** Download any necessary travel apps before your trip, such as maps, language translation, and local guides. Offline maps can be particularly useful, as cell service may be spotty in more remote areas of the island. Google Maps or an offline GPS app can help you navigate Lipari's winding streets and trails.
- **E-Reader or Books:** If you enjoy reading, an e-reader loaded with books is a space-saving option. Alternatively, bring a paperback or two for some beachside relaxation.

Health and Hygiene Items

- **Personal Medications:** If you take prescription medications, ensure you have enough to last your entire trip, plus a few extra days in case of delays. Bring a copy of your prescription, especially if you're carrying controlled substances. Pack your medications in their original packaging to avoid any issues at customs.
- **First Aid Kit:** A small first aid kit with essentials like adhesive bandages, antiseptic wipes, pain relievers, and motion sickness tablets can be invaluable. Include any personal items like blister pads if you plan to hike or walk extensively.
- **Toiletries:** While you can find most basic toiletries on Lipari, it's a good idea to bring travel-sized versions of your preferred products. This includes items like shampoo,

conditioner, body wash, toothpaste, and deodorant. Don't forget sunscreen, insect repellent, and after-sun lotion for any post-beach care.
- **Hand Sanitizer and Wipes:** Hand sanitizer and disinfectant wipes are useful for maintaining hygiene, especially in public places or when using public transportation. These items are particularly handy when visiting busy tourist spots.

Travel Documents and Essentials

- **Passport and ID:** Your passport is the most important document you'll need for international travel. Make sure it's valid for at least six months beyond your planned departure date. If you're an EU citizen, a valid national ID card may suffice. Keep a photocopy or digital copy of your passport in a separate location in case it's lost or stolen.
- **Travel Insurance Documents:** Bring copies of your travel insurance policy, including the emergency contact numbers for your insurer. Having these documents easily accessible can be a lifesaver in the event of an emergency.
- **Tickets and Reservations:** Print out copies of your flight tickets, ferry bookings, accommodation confirmations, and any pre-booked tours or activities. While digital copies on your phone are convenient, having a paper backup can be helpful if your device runs out of battery or you have issues with connectivity.
- **Money and Cards:** Bring a mix of payment methods, including credit cards, debit cards, and some cash in Euros for smaller purchases or places that don't accept cards. It's a good idea to inform your bank of your travel plans to avoid any issues with card transactions abroad. A money

belt or neck pouch can help keep your valuables secure while you're out and about.

Miscellaneous Items

- **Daypack or Backpack:** A small daypack is essential for carrying your daily essentials, such as water, sunscreen, camera, and snacks. Look for a lightweight, durable option with multiple compartments for organization. A waterproof or water-resistant bag can be particularly useful if you're planning any boat trips or beach outings.
- **Reusable Shopping Bag:** Many places in Italy charge for plastic bags, so a reusable shopping bag is handy for any shopping trips, whether for groceries, souvenirs, or beach supplies. It's also environmentally friendly, helping you reduce your plastic footprint while traveling.
- **Language Guide or Phrasebook:** While many people in Lipari speak English, especially in tourist areas, having a basic understanding of Italian can enhance your experience. A small phrasebook or a language app can help you navigate menus, ask for directions, and interact with locals.
- **Portable Safe or Lock:** If you're staying in shared accommodations or simply want added security, a portable travel safe or a small lock for your luggage can provide peace of mind. This is especially useful for securing your passport, money, and other valuables when you're away from your accommodation.

Seasonal and Activity-Specific Items

- **Hiking Gear:** If you're planning to explore Lipari's hiking trails, bring appropriate gear. This includes a comfortable

backpack, a hydration system or water bottle, hiking boots or sturdy shoes, a hat, and sun protection. Trekking poles can also be useful on more challenging paths.
- **Winter Travel:** If you're visiting Lipari in the winter, pack warmer layers, including a fleece or wool sweater, a windproof jacket, and a beanie or gloves. While the weather is generally mild, evenings can be cool, and it's best to be prepared for occasional rain.
- **Boat and Water Activities:** For boat trips, pack a waterproof bag or dry sack to protect your belongings from splashes. If you're prone to seasickness, consider bringing motion sickness tablets or wristbands. A waterproof phone case is also useful for taking photos or navigating while on the water.

By carefully considering your packing list and tailoring it to your specific plans and the season of your visit, you can ensure a comfortable and enjoyable trip to Lipari. With the right gear and essentials, you'll be well-prepared to explore all that this beautiful island has to offer, from its stunning beaches to its charming villages and rugged landscapes.

NAVIGATING LIPARI

Exploring Lipari is quite simple thanks to its manageable size and accessible transportation options. Here's how you can make the most of your travels around the island.

Using Public Transport

- **Local Buses:** Lipari's local bus network provides an efficient and cost-effective way to travel between the main town, various villages, and popular beaches. Although bus routes are limited and schedules might vary, especially during the off-season, they're a reliable option for getting around. It's helpful to check the latest timetables and plan your trips accordingly.
- **Taxis:** Taxis are readily available on Lipari and can be flagged down on the street or pre-booked. They're especially useful for reaching areas not covered by the bus routes or for quick trips, particularly if you're carrying luggage. Taxis are also convenient for short journeys within the main town.

Renting Vehicles

- **Scooters:** Renting a scooter is a favored choice among visitors for exploring Lipari. Scooters offer great flexibility and allow you to easily access more remote beaches and scenic villages. Rental services are widely available in the main town, and the cost is usually reasonable. Be sure to have a valid driver's license and familiarize yourself with the local traffic rules.

- **Cars:** For those who prefer more comfort, car rentals are available on the island. Renting a car is ideal if you're traveling with family or planning to explore further afield. Cars provide the benefit of air conditioning and additional space for luggage. Just be mindful of parking options at your accommodation and adhere to local driving regulations.

Walking and Biking

- **Walking:** The main town of Lipari is compact and easily walkable, making it perfect for exploring on foot. Many attractions, shops, and eateries are within a short stroll of each other, allowing you to soak up the local charm and vibrant atmosphere at your own pace.
- **Cycling:** Renting a bicycle is another eco-friendly way to see Lipari. Cycling offers a leisurely way to experience the island's beautiful landscapes and coastal roads. Keep in mind that the terrain can be hilly, so it's important to be prepared for some challenging rides. Don't forget to bring water and sun protection for your journey.

Boating Options

- **Boat Tours:** Given Lipari's island setting, boat tours are a fantastic way to explore neighboring islands and hidden coves. You can join organized excursions departing from the main port that visit other Aeolian Islands like Stromboli and Vulcano or take a scenic tour around Lipari itself. It's advisable to book these trips ahead of time, especially during the busy summer months.

- **Ferries:** Ferries are the primary means of traveling to and from Lipari, connecting the island with Sicily and other Aeolian Islands. Regular ferry services operate from Milazzo in Sicily, offering stunning views of the surrounding sea and islands during the journey. Be sure to check ferry schedules and purchase tickets in advance, particularly during peak travel periods.

Taxi Boats

- **Private Water Taxis:** For a more personalized experience on the water, consider hiring a private water taxi. These boats can be arranged through local providers and offer flexible schedules and destinations. Water taxis are ideal for reaching secluded beaches or organizing private group outings tailored to your preferences.

By choosing the right transportation method for your needs, getting around Lipari is both convenient and enjoyable. Whether you're cruising the island's coast on a scooter, strolling through town, or embarking on a boat adventure, exploring Lipari is a delightful experience.

Transportation Options in Lipari: Buses, Taxis, and Car Rentals

Understanding these options—buses, taxis, and car rentals—will allow you to navigate the island efficiently and enjoyably.

Buses: A Cost-Effective and Convenient Choice

- **Routes and Coverage:** The main bus routes link the town of Lipari with key destinations such as Canneto, Acquacalda, and Pianoconte. These buses are particularly useful for reaching beaches, hiking trails, and other attractions. While the bus service covers most of the island, some remote areas might not be accessible by public transport, making alternative options necessary.
- **Fares and Tickets:** Bus fares on Lipari are inexpensive, making this a budget-friendly option for travelers. Tickets can usually be purchased directly from the driver or at designated kiosks in town. It's advisable to carry small change, as drivers may not always have enough to break larger bills.
- **Considerations:** While buses are a great option for many, they can be crowded during peak tourist season, and service frequency may decrease in the evening or off-season. If you're planning to rely on buses, it's a good idea to plan your itinerary around the bus schedule to avoid long waits.

Taxis: Flexible and Convenient

- **Taxi Services:** Taxis are widely available on Lipari, offering a flexible and convenient way to travel around the island, particularly if you're carrying luggage or traveling in a group. Taxis can be hailed on the street in the main town, found at taxi stands, or booked in advance by phone or through your hotel.
- **Cost and Payment:** Taxi fares on Lipari are generally more expensive than the bus, but they offer the advantage of door-to-door service and greater flexibility in terms of timing and destination. It's common to agree on a fare before starting the journey, especially for longer trips or

when traveling to less frequented areas. Most taxis accept cash, and some may accept credit cards, but it's always good to confirm before the trip begins.
- **Special Services:** In addition to standard taxi rides, some taxi services offer personalized tours of the island, taking you to lesser-known sites and providing local insights along the way. This can be a great option if you're short on time or prefer a more guided experience.
- **Considerations:** Taxis are particularly useful if you're traveling late at night or to destinations not served by the bus routes. However, during the busy tourist season, it may be harder to find an available taxi on short notice, so pre-booking is recommended for important journeys.

Car Rentals: Freedom to Explore at Your Own Pace

- **Rental Options:** Renting a car on Lipari gives you the freedom to explore the island at your own pace, without being tied to public transport schedules. Several car rental agencies operate in the main town, offering a range of vehicles from compact cars to larger family vehicles. Renting a car is especially advantageous if you plan to visit more remote parts of the island or if you're traveling with a lot of luggage.
- **Driving Conditions:** The roads on Lipari are generally well-maintained, but they can be narrow and winding, particularly in the more rural areas. Drivers should be prepared for steep inclines and sharp bends. Parking can also be challenging in the main town during peak season, so it's advisable to check whether your accommodation provides parking facilities.

- **Rental Requirements:** To rent a car on Lipari, you'll need a valid driver's license. An International Driving Permit (IDP) may be required if your license is not in Italian or does not use the Latin alphabet. Most rental companies require drivers to be at least 21 years old, and drivers under 25 may face additional fees.
- **Cost and Fuel:** The cost of renting a car on Lipari varies depending on the season, type of vehicle, and rental duration. It's often more economical to book in advance, especially during the high season. Fuel is readily available, but gas stations may be scarce outside of the main town, so it's a good idea to refuel whenever you have the opportunity.
- **Considerations:** While a rental car provides flexibility, it's important to consider the environmental impact and potential stress of navigating unfamiliar roads. If you're planning to explore only the main town and nearby areas, you might find that public transportation or taxis are sufficient and more convenient.

Choosing the Right Option for You

The best transportation option for getting around Lipari depends on your travel style, budget, and itinerary. Buses are ideal for budget-conscious travelers looking to explore the island's main attractions. Taxis offer convenience and flexibility, especially for short trips or when public transport isn't available. Renting a car is the best choice for those who want complete freedom to explore at their own pace, particularly if you're planning to visit more remote areas.

No matter which option you choose, navigating Lipari is generally straightforward and enjoyable, allowing you to experience all the beauty and charm this island has to offer.

Walking and Biking Routes in Lipari

Exploring Lipari on foot or by bike is one of the most rewarding ways to experience the island's natural beauty, historical sites, and breathtaking coastal views. If you're an avid hiker, a casual walker, or a cycling enthusiast, Lipari offers a variety of trails and routes that cater to different levels of fitness and interest. Here's a guide to some of the best walking and biking routes on the island.

Walking Routes: Discover Lipari on Foot

Walking is an excellent way to immerse yourself in the landscapes, culture, and history of Lipari. The island's trails range from easy coastal walks to more challenging hikes that take you to higher elevations with panoramic views.

- **The Lipari Town Historical Walk:** This leisurely route takes you through the charming streets of Lipari Town, where you can explore the island's rich history. Starting at the Marina Corta, you can visit the impressive Lipari Castle, which houses the Aeolian Archaeological Museum. As you wander through the town, you'll pass by traditional houses, local shops, and churches, offering a glimpse into the daily life of the island's residents. This walk is perfect for those interested in history and culture, and it's easily accessible for all fitness levels.
- **Quattrocchi Viewpoint Hike:** For those seeking stunning vistas, the hike to Quattrocchi Viewpoint is a must. This moderate trail starts near Lipari Town and takes you along

a scenic route overlooking the sea and neighboring islands. The viewpoint offers spectacular views of the rugged coastline, with the island of Vulcano visible in the distance. The hike is approximately 4 kilometers round trip and is suitable for most hikers, although the terrain can be uneven in places.
- **Monte Guardia Trail:** This more challenging hike takes you to the summit of Monte Guardia, the highest point on Lipari. The trail begins near the town and ascends through lush vegetation and volcanic terrain. At the top, you'll be rewarded with 360-degree views of the Aeolian Islands and the surrounding Tyrrhenian Sea. The hike is about 7 kilometers round trip and is best suited for experienced hikers due to its steep sections and rocky paths.
- **Canneto Beach Walk:** If you prefer a more relaxed walk, the route from Lipari Town to Canneto Beach is a pleasant option. This flat, easy walk takes you along the coast, with beautiful views of the sea and the chance to stop at several small beaches along the way. The walk is about 3 kilometers each way, and once you reach Canneto, you can enjoy the beach or visit one of the local cafes for refreshments.
- **Pianoconte to San Calogero:** This route takes you from the village of Pianoconte to the ancient thermal baths at San Calogero. The trail is moderately difficult and leads you through rural landscapes, olive groves, and vineyards. Along the way, you'll encounter remnants of Lipari's volcanic history and enjoy peaceful countryside views. The walk is about 5 kilometers round trip and offers a unique combination of nature and history.

Biking Routes

Cycling around Lipari is an exhilarating way to cover more ground and explore the island's diverse landscapes. While some routes can be challenging due to the island's hilly terrain, there are also gentler options for less experienced cyclists.

- **Lipari Coastal Loop:** This popular biking route circles the island, offering a comprehensive tour of Lipari's coastline. Starting from Lipari Town, the route follows the coastal roads, passing through villages like Canneto and Acquacalda. Along the way, you'll encounter stunning views of the sea, rocky cliffs, and beaches. The loop is approximately 25 kilometers and includes a mix of flat sections and challenging climbs. This route is suitable for experienced cyclists looking for a full-day adventure.
- **Canneto to Acquacalda Ride:** For a shorter and less demanding ride, the route from Canneto to Acquacalda is ideal. This 10-kilometer stretch follows the northeastern coast of Lipari, offering scenic views of the turquoise waters and black sand beaches. The road is relatively flat, making it accessible for most cyclists, and you can stop in Acquacalda to relax by the sea or enjoy a meal at a local restaurant.
- **Monte Pelato Circuit:** This route takes you on a challenging ride through the island's interior, including a climb up Monte Pelato, one of Lipari's volcanic hills. The trail starts in Lipari Town and heads inland, passing through vineyards and forested areas. The ascent to Monte Pelato is steep and requires good cycling skills, but the panoramic views from the top are worth the effort. The circuit is around 15 kilometers and is best suited for experienced mountain bikers.

- **Pianoconte to Quattrocchi:** This moderate route offers a mix of coastal and inland scenery, starting from the village of Pianoconte and heading towards the Quattrocchi Viewpoint. The ride includes some gentle climbs and descents, making it a good option for cyclists with moderate experience. The total distance is about 12 kilometers round trip, and the route offers plenty of opportunities to stop and take in the views.
- **Exploring Southern Lipari:** The southern part of Lipari offers quieter roads and stunning natural landscapes, perfect for a peaceful bike ride. Start in Lipari Town and head south towards the villages of Pianogreca and Serra. The route takes you through rolling hills and past traditional farms, with occasional views of the sea. This area is less developed, providing a tranquil cycling experience. The distance can vary depending on how far you wish to explore, but a round trip of 20 kilometers is typical.

Tips for Walking and Biking in Lipari

- **Prepare for the Terrain:** Lipari's terrain can be hilly and rocky, so it's important to wear appropriate footwear for walking and ensure your bike is in good condition. If you're planning a longer hike or ride, bring plenty of water, snacks, and sun protection.
- **Respect the Environment:** The natural beauty of Lipari is one of its greatest assets, so be sure to follow the Leave No Trace principles. Stick to marked trails, avoid disturbing wildlife, and carry out all trash.
- **Plan for the Weather:** The weather on Lipari can be hot, especially in summer, so plan your activities for the cooler

parts of the day, such as early morning or late afternoon. Check the weather forecast before heading out, particularly if you're planning a longer excursion.
- **Stay Safe:** If you're cycling, always wear a helmet and be cautious on steep descents. Roads can be narrow, and traffic may include other cyclists, cars, and pedestrians. For walking, consider carrying a map or using a GPS device to ensure you stay on track, as some trails may not be well-marked.

Ferry Services to Neighboring Islands: Exploring the Aeolian Archipelago

Lipari serves as a hub for ferry services to its neighboring islands. These ferries offer a convenient and scenic way to explore the other islands, each with its unique charm, landscapes, and attractions.

Overview of Ferry Services

Ferries are the primary mode of transportation between the Aeolian Islands, providing regular and reliable connections. The main ferry operators include Liberty Lines and Siremar, both of which offer high-speed hydrofoils and larger ferries. These services vary in frequency depending on the season, with more frequent crossings during the summer months when tourism peaks.

- **Hydrofoils vs. Traditional Ferries:** Hydrofoils are faster and typically used for shorter trips between the islands, making them ideal for day trips or quick transfers. Traditional ferries are slower but can accommodate

vehicles and larger groups, offering a more leisurely journey with the option to bring your car or scooter.
- **Booking Tickets:** Tickets for ferries can be purchased at the port, online through the ferry operators' websites, or through local travel agencies. It's advisable to book in advance during the high season to ensure availability, especially for hydrofoils which can fill up quickly.

Ferry Routes to Neighboring Islands

Each neighboring island offers distinct attractions, from active volcanoes to secluded beaches and charming villages. Here's a look at the most popular ferry routes from Lipari:

- **Lipari to Vulcano:**
    - **Journey Duration:** Approximately 10-20 minutes by hydrofoil.
    - **Highlights:** Vulcano, known for its active volcano, offers visitors the chance to hike to the crater for stunning views, relax in therapeutic mud baths, and enjoy black sand beaches. The ferry ride from Lipari is short, making it a perfect day trip destination.
    - **Frequency:** Multiple daily departures, with increased frequency during peak season.
- **Lipari to Salina:**
    - **Journey Duration:** Approximately 30-40 minutes by hydrofoil.
    - **Highlights:** Salina, the greenest of the Aeolian Islands, is famous for its vineyards, caper production, and the twin peaks of Monte Fossa delle Felci and Monte dei Porri. The island offers excellent opportunities for hiking, wine tasting, and exploring charming villages like Santa Marina and Malfa.
    - **Frequency:** Several daily services, with options to visit different ports on Salina.
- **Lipari to Panarea:**
    - **Journey Duration:** Approximately 45-60 minutes by hydrofoil.

- **Highlights:** Panarea is the smallest and most exclusive of the Aeolian Islands, known for its chic atmosphere, beautiful beaches, and vibrant nightlife. Visitors can explore the prehistoric village of Cala Junco, enjoy snorkeling in crystal-clear waters, or simply relax in the island's stylish cafes.
  - **Frequency:** Regular services throughout the day, particularly popular in the summer.
- **Lipari to Stromboli:**
  - **Journey Duration:** Approximately 1 hour 15 minutes by hydrofoil.
  - **Highlights:** Stromboli is renowned for its active volcano, which has been erupting continuously for over 2,000 years. The island is a top destination for adventure seekers who can hike to the crater to witness the spectacular eruptions or take a boat tour around the island to view the "Sciara del Fuoco" (Stream of Fire).
  - **Frequency:** Multiple departures daily, with evening services available for those wishing to see the volcano's nighttime eruptions.
- **Lipari to Filicudi and Alicudi:**
  - **Journey Duration:** Filicudi (2 hours) and Alicudi (2 hours 30 minutes) by hydrofoil.
  - **Highlights:** Filicudi and Alicudi are the most remote and least developed of the Aeolian Islands, offering a peaceful escape from the crowds. Filicudi is known for its rugged landscapes, ancient ruins, and the Grotta del Bue Marino, a stunning sea cave. Alicudi, the westernmost island, is a haven for those

seeking tranquility, with its steep terrain and traditional, slow-paced lifestyle.
  - **Frequency:** Less frequent services, typically once or twice a day, making these islands ideal for overnight stays rather than day trips.

Practical Tips for Ferry Travel

- **Seasonal Variations:** Ferry schedules vary significantly between the high and low seasons. During the summer, ferries operate more frequently, and additional routes may be available. In the off-season, services are reduced, and weather conditions can occasionally cause delays or cancellations.
- **Travel Time Considerations:** While the journey times for hydrofoils are generally shorter, traditional ferries offer a more relaxed experience with the ability to carry vehicles. Consider your schedule and preferences when choosing between the two.
- **Luggage:** Most ferries allow passengers to bring a reasonable amount of luggage without extra charges, but it's a good idea to check with the operator if you have large or unusual items. Hydrofoils have more limited space, so pack accordingly if you're traveling on one.
- **Comfort and Amenities:** Hydrofoils and ferries typically offer basic amenities such as seating, restrooms, and in some cases, small cafes or snack bars. It's advisable to bring water, snacks, and any necessary travel items, especially on longer routes or if you're traveling with children.
- **Accessibility:** Most ferry services are accessible to passengers with limited mobility, but it's recommended to

inform the ferry operator in advance if you require assistance. Some smaller or older vessels may have more limited accessibility features.

ACCOMMODATION OPTIONS

When it comes to choosing accommodation in Lipari, the island offers a wide array of options that cater to different tastes, budgets, and travel styles. If you're looking for luxurious hotels, cozy bed and breakfasts, or self-catering apartments, Lipari has something for everyone. Here's a guide to help you find the perfect place to stay during your visit.

Types of Accommodation

Luxury Hotels and Resorts in Lipari

For those who seek a touch of luxury, Lipari boasts several upscale hotels that provide not just a place to stay, but a full experience of comfort and elegance. These hotels often feature amenities such as swimming pools, spas, fine dining restaurants, and stunning views of the sea or surrounding landscapes. Staying at one of these properties allows you to unwind in style after a day of exploring, with services designed to cater to your every need.

Top Luxury Hotels and Resorts

1. **Hotel Villa Enrica**
    - **Location:** Overlooking the bay of Marina Lunga, Hotel Villa Enrica offers a serene retreat with breathtaking views of the Tyrrhenian Sea.
    - **Amenities:** This boutique hotel features an infinity pool surrounded by lush gardens, elegantly

decorated rooms with private terraces, and an on-site restaurant serving gourmet Aeolian cuisine. The hotel's design blends traditional Mediterranean architecture with modern comforts, creating a peaceful and luxurious ambiance.
- o **Highlights:** Guests can enjoy personalized service, including private boat tours, in-room massages, and tailored excursions to the surrounding islands. The tranquil setting and stunning views make it an ideal choice for couples seeking a romantic getaway.

2. **Therasia Resort Sea & Spa**
    - o **Location:** Perched on the cliffs of the neighboring island of Vulcano, just a short ferry ride from Lipari, Therasia Resort Sea & Spa offers unparalleled luxury and panoramic views of the Aeolian archipelago.
    - o **Amenities:** The resort boasts several infinity pools, a full-service spa offering treatments with local volcanic products, and multiple dining options, including a Michelin-starred restaurant. Rooms and suites are spacious, with private balconies or terraces overlooking the sea.
    - o **Highlights:** Therasia Resort is a haven for wellness and relaxation, with an extensive spa menu, yoga classes, and a private beach. The resort also offers exclusive excursions, including sunset boat trips and guided hikes to Vulcano's crater.

3. **Hotel Mea**
    - o **Location:** Situated close to Lipari Town, Hotel Mea provides luxury in a convenient location, just a short walk from the harbor and the historic center.

- **Amenities:** The hotel features a beautiful Mediterranean garden, a panoramic swimming pool, and a stylish restaurant offering local and international cuisine. Rooms are decorated in a chic, contemporary style, with some offering sea views and private terraces.
- **Highlights:** Hotel Mea is known for its warm hospitality and attention to detail. Guests can enjoy customized experiences, such as private wine tastings, cooking classes, and guided tours of the island's archaeological sites.

4. **Hotel Tritone**
    - **Location:** Nestled in a quiet area just outside Lipari Town, Hotel Tritone combines luxury with a peaceful atmosphere, making it a perfect retreat for relaxation.
    - **Amenities:** The hotel offers a large outdoor pool with hydromassage jets, a wellness center with a sauna and Turkish bath, and a fine dining restaurant with a focus on fresh, local ingredients. Rooms are spacious and elegantly furnished, with balconies or terraces.
    - **Highlights:** Hotel Tritone is known for its extensive wine cellar and offers wine pairing dinners, where guests can enjoy local and international wines with gourmet meals. The hotel also arranges private boat excursions and diving trips, allowing guests to explore the Aeolian sea in style.

5. **Residence La Giara**
    - **Location:** Close to the heart of Lipari Town, Residence La Giara offers luxurious apartment-style

accommodations, ideal for travelers who value both comfort and independence.
- ○ **Amenities:** The residence features a beautiful garden with a swimming pool, and each apartment includes a fully equipped kitchen, a living area, and a private terrace or balcony. The decor combines modern elegance with traditional Aeolian touches.
- ○ **Highlights:** Residence La Giara is perfect for families or groups looking for a more personalized and private experience. Guests can enjoy the convenience of a self-catering apartment while still benefiting from hotel-style services, such as daily housekeeping, breakfast delivery, and concierge assistance.

Luxury Experiences and Services

- **Private Transfers and Excursions:** Many luxury hotels in Lipari offer private transfers from the mainland or other islands, ensuring a seamless and stress-free arrival. They also arrange exclusive excursions, such as private yacht charters, helicopter tours, and guided hikes, allowing you to explore the Aeolian Islands in style.
- **Gourmet Dining:** Fine dining is a key feature of luxury hotels in Lipari. Many establishments boast on-site restaurants that focus on gourmet Aeolian cuisine, often with a contemporary twist. These restaurants typically use fresh, local ingredients, including seafood, capers, and Malvasia wine. Some hotels even offer cooking classes where guests can learn to prepare traditional dishes.
- **Wellness and Relaxation:** Spa services are a hallmark of Lipari's luxury hotels, with many offering full-service

wellness centers that include saunas, steam rooms, and massage treatments. These services often incorporate local products, such as volcanic mud and sea salt, enhancing the connection to the island's natural resources.
- **Tailored Services:** Luxury hotels in Lipari pride themselves on offering personalized services. Whether it's arranging a private dinner on your terrace, organizing a bespoke island tour, or providing in-room spa treatments, these hotels go above and beyond to cater to your individual preferences.

Booking Your Luxury Stay

- **Seasonal Considerations:** The high season in Lipari runs from June to September, and luxury hotels tend to book up quickly during this time. It's advisable to book your accommodation well in advance to secure your preferred dates and room type.
- **Exclusive Offers:** Many luxury hotels offer special packages or deals, particularly in the shoulder seasons (spring and fall). These might include discounted rates, complimentary spa treatments, or added extras like a bottle of local wine upon arrival.
- **Tailored Recommendations:** If you have specific preferences or interests, don't hesitate to contact the hotel in advance. Many luxury hotels are happy to tailor your experience, whether that means arranging for a specific room, preparing for special dietary needs, or planning a unique activity.

Staying at a luxury hotel or resort in Lipari ensures an unforgettable experience, where every detail is designed for comfort, relaxation, and indulgence. From the stunning views to the impeccable service, these accommodations provide the perfect base for exploring the beauty and charm of the Aeolian Islands.

Boutique Hotels and Bed & Breakfasts in Lipari

For travelers seeking a more intimate and personalized experience, Lipari offers a variety of boutique hotels and bed & breakfast (B&B) accommodations. These smaller establishments combine the charm and character of the island with a warm, welcoming atmosphere, often providing a more local and authentic experience.

Boutique Hotels

Boutique hotels in Lipari are known for their distinct style, attention to detail, and personalized service. These hotels often feature fewer rooms than larger properties, allowing for a more intimate and tailored experience.

1. **Hotel Villa Meligunis**
    - **Location:** Nestled in the historic center of Lipari Town, Hotel Villa Meligunis is set in an elegant 18th-century villa, offering guests a blend of history and modern comfort.
    - **Ambiance:** The hotel's decor reflects the rich cultural heritage of the island, with antique furnishings, local artwork, and a warm, inviting atmosphere. The rooftop terrace provides stunning views of the harbor and the sea, making it a perfect spot for breakfast or evening cocktails.
    - **Service:** With its small size, the hotel prides itself on providing personalized service, ensuring each guest feels at home. The staff can arrange private

tours, boat excursions, and other activities tailored to your interests.

2. **Albergo Boutique Casajanca**
   - **Location:** Situated in the village of Canneto, just a short distance from Lipari Town, Albergo Boutique Casajanca offers a tranquil setting with easy access to the beach.
   - **Ambiance:** The hotel is housed in a historic building with a charming courtyard garden. The rooms are individually decorated, combining traditional Aeolian style with modern comforts. Some rooms feature private balconies or terraces overlooking the garden or the sea.
   - **Service:** The owners of Casajanca take great pride in offering a personal touch, with homemade breakfasts, local tips, and a welcoming environment that makes guests feel like part of the family.
3. **Hotel Carasco**
   - **Location:** Perched on a cliff just outside the main town, Hotel Carasco offers breathtaking views of the sea and the neighboring islands, providing a serene and secluded atmosphere.
   - **Ambiance:** The hotel combines the elegance of a traditional Mediterranean villa with contemporary amenities. The spacious rooms are decorated in a classic style, and the hotel features a private beach, an outdoor pool, and a restaurant serving gourmet Aeolian cuisine.
   - **Service:** Guests at Hotel Carasco enjoy a high level of service, with options for private dinners, personalized wellness treatments, and exclusive boat tours to explore the surrounding islands.

Bed & Breakfasts

B&Bs in Lipari offer a homely and authentic experience, often run by local families who provide a warm welcome and insider knowledge of the island. These accommodations are perfect for travelers who want to immerse themselves in the local culture.

1. **B&B Il Cappero**
    - **Location:** Located in the peaceful area of Quattropani, B&B Il Cappero offers stunning views of the sea and nearby islands, making it an ideal retreat for those seeking tranquility.
    - **Ambiance:** The B&B features just a few rooms, each uniquely decorated with rustic charm and modern comforts. The surrounding gardens and terraces are perfect for relaxing with a book or enjoying a sunset aperitivo.
    - **Service:** The hosts of Il Cappero go out of their way to make guests feel at home, offering a delicious homemade breakfast each morning, featuring local products and traditional Aeolian pastries. They also provide helpful tips on exploring the island and can arrange guided tours and activities.
2. **B&B La Villetta**
    - **Location:** Situated in the village of Pianoconte, B&B La Villetta offers a rural setting with beautiful views of Lipari's countryside and the sea.
    - **Ambiance:** The B&B is set in a traditional Aeolian house, with rooms that reflect the island's heritage through their decor and furnishings. The large garden, filled with Mediterranean plants and

flowers, is a peaceful retreat where guests can relax and unwind.
- **Service:** Guests at La Villetta are treated like family, with the hosts providing a warm and welcoming environment. Breakfast is served on the terrace, and the hosts are happy to share their knowledge of the island, offering recommendations for local restaurants, hikes, and beaches.

3. **B&B Il Gelso**
   - **Location:** Just a short walk from the beach in Canneto, B&B Il Gelso is a charming and cozy retreat that offers easy access to both the sea and the town.
   - **Ambiance:** The B&B is named after the ancient mulberry tree (gelso) that shades the garden, providing a serene and shaded space for guests to relax. The rooms are decorated in a simple yet elegant style, with some featuring balconies or terraces with sea views.
   - **Service:** The owners of Il Gelso are known for their hospitality and attention to detail. They serve a delicious breakfast each morning, including freshly baked goods, and are always available to help with travel arrangements or recommendations for local attractions.

4. **B&B Casa Mafalda**
   - **Location:** Centrally located in Lipari Town, B&B Casa Mafalda offers a convenient base for exploring the island, with the main square, shops, and restaurants just a short stroll away.

- **Ambiance:** The B&B features bright, airy rooms decorated in a traditional Aeolian style, with a focus on comfort and simplicity. The rooftop terrace offers panoramic views of the town and the sea, providing a perfect spot to enjoy breakfast or an evening drink.
- **Service:** Casa Mafalda is praised for its friendly and accommodating hosts, who go above and beyond to ensure guests have an enjoyable stay. The hosts are happy to arrange boat trips, tours, and other activities, making sure guests get the most out of their visit to Lipari.

Choosing the Right Boutique Hotel or B&B

- **Location:** Consider the location that best suits your plans. If you want to be close to the action, staying in or near Lipari Town is ideal. For a quieter experience, look for accommodations in areas like Canneto, Pianoconte, or Quattropani.
- **Style and Atmosphere:** Each boutique hotel and B&B has its own unique style and ambiance, so choose one that matches your preferences. Whether you prefer a historic villa, a rustic countryside retreat, or a modern beachfront property, Lipari has options to suit every taste.
- **Personalized Service:** One of the main advantages of staying in a boutique hotel or B&B is the personalized service. Many of these establishments are family-run, offering a more personal touch than larger hotels. Don't hesitate to communicate your preferences or special requests in advance to enhance your stay.

Booking Tips

- **Advance Booking:** Boutique hotels and B&Bs often have limited availability due to their small size, so it's advisable to book early, especially during peak tourist season.
- **Seasonal Offers:** Keep an eye out for special offers, particularly in the shoulder seasons when some accommodations may provide discounts or additional perks.
- **Guest Reviews:** Reading reviews from previous guests can give you a good sense of what to expect, from the quality of service to the atmosphere and amenities.

Staying in a boutique hotel or B&B in Lipari allows you to experience the island in a more intimate and authentic way, with personalized service and unique accommodations that reflect the character and charm of the Aeolian Islands.

Budget Accommodation and Hostels in Lipari

For travelers on a budget, Lipari offers a variety of affordable accommodation options that don't compromise on comfort or convenience. If you're a backpacker, a student, or simply looking to save on lodging, you'll find hostels, guesthouses, and budget hotels that provide clean, comfortable, and friendly places to stay. Here's a detailed guide to the budget-friendly accommodations in Lipari.

Budget Hotels

Budget hotels in Lipari offer a cost-effective way to enjoy the island while providing essential amenities and services. These hotels typically feature clean, comfortable rooms and are often located near the main attractions, making them an excellent choice for budget-conscious travelers who still want a convenient and pleasant stay.

1. **Hotel La Zagara**
    - **Location:** Located in Canneto, just a short walk from the beach, Hotel La Zagara offers affordable accommodation with easy access to the sea and local restaurants.
    - **Ambiance:** The hotel features simple yet comfortable rooms, many with balconies offering views of the sea or the surrounding hills. The decor is minimalistic but functional, ensuring a comfortable stay without unnecessary frills.
    - **Amenities:** Guests can enjoy a complimentary breakfast each morning, and the hotel provides free Wi-Fi, air conditioning, and a small garden area for relaxation. The staff is friendly and always ready to assist with any needs or travel arrangements.
2. **Hotel Oriente**
    - **Location:** Situated in the heart of Lipari Town, Hotel Oriente is a budget-friendly hotel that offers easy access to shops, restaurants, and the ferry terminal.
    - **Ambiance:** The hotel has a traditional Aeolian style, with simple, cozy rooms that are well-maintained and equipped with all the basics needed for a comfortable stay. The common areas, including a small courtyard, offer a pleasant place to unwind after a day of exploring.
    - **Amenities:** Hotel Oriente offers a complimentary breakfast, free Wi-Fi, and a 24-hour front desk. The

central location makes it a convenient base for exploring the island, and the staff can help with recommendations and bookings for local tours and activities.

Hostels

Hostels in Lipari provide a budget-friendly option for solo travelers, backpackers, and anyone looking to meet fellow travelers. These accommodations are typically more social, with shared spaces and sometimes even shared rooms, making them a great choice for those who value both economy and community.

1. **Oasi d'Oriente Hostel**
   - **Location:** Located in Canneto, Oasi d'Oriente Hostel is close to the beach and provides a relaxed, friendly atmosphere for budget travelers.
   - **Ambiance:** The hostel offers both private rooms and dormitory-style accommodations, all of which are clean, simple, and comfortable. The communal areas include a shared kitchen, a lounge, and an outdoor terrace where guests can socialize or relax.
   - **Amenities:** Guests can take advantage of free Wi-Fi, luggage storage, and a communal kitchen where they can prepare their own meals. The hostel also organizes social events, such as group dinners and excursions, making it easy to meet other travelers.
2. **Hostel Agave**
   - **Location:** Situated in the center of Lipari Town, Hostel Agave is an ideal spot for those looking to explore the town's historic sites and vibrant nightlife on a budget.

- **Ambiance:** The hostel is set in a traditional building with a cozy, welcoming vibe. It offers a mix of private rooms and shared dorms, all with basic but comfortable furnishings. The common areas include a small garden and a lounge where guests can hang out and share stories of their adventures.
- **Amenities:** Hostel Agave provides free Wi-Fi, a communal kitchen, and a complimentary light breakfast. The hostel staff is known for being friendly and helpful, offering tips on the best places to visit and how to get around the island.

Guesthouses

Guesthouses in Lipari offer a home-away-from-home experience at an affordable price. These small, family-run establishments provide a more personal touch, with hosts who are often eager to share their local knowledge and ensure guests have an enjoyable stay.

1. **Casa Matarazzo**
   - **Location:** Located in the historic center of Lipari Town, Casa Matarazzo offers budget-friendly accommodations in a charming, family-run guesthouse.
   - **Ambiance:** The guesthouse features a handful of rooms, each individually decorated with simple, comfortable furnishings. The atmosphere is warm and inviting, making guests feel like they're staying with family.
   - **Amenities:** Casa Matarazzo provides free Wi-Fi, air conditioning, and a continental breakfast each

morning. The hosts are known for their hospitality, often going out of their way to ensure guests have a memorable stay.

2. **Pensione Neri**
    - **Location:** Situated in the quiet village of Acquacalda, Pensione Neri offers a peaceful retreat away from the more touristy areas, perfect for those looking for a more laid-back experience.
    - **Ambiance:** This guesthouse is known for its simple, rustic charm, with basic but clean and comfortable rooms. The atmosphere is very relaxed, with a focus on creating a homely environment where guests can unwind and enjoy the slower pace of island life.
    - **Amenities:** Guests at Pensione Neri can enjoy a traditional Aeolian breakfast, as well as free Wi-Fi and a communal garden area. The guesthouse is close to the beach and offers stunning views of the sea and surrounding mountains.

Tips for Budget Travelers in Lipari

- **Book in Advance:** Budget accommodations, especially hostels and guesthouses, can fill up quickly during the high season. Booking in advance ensures you secure a place to stay at the best possible rate.
- **Travel Off-Peak:** Visiting Lipari during the shoulder seasons (spring and fall) can help you find lower rates and avoid the crowds. Many budget accommodations offer discounts during these times.
- **Self-Catering:** If you're staying at a hostel or guesthouse with kitchen facilities, consider preparing some of your own meals. This can significantly reduce your daily expenses, especially if you take advantage of local markets for fresh produce.

- **Use Public Transport:** Lipari has a reliable public bus system that connects most parts of the island. Using public transport instead of taxis or car rentals can help you save money on getting around.
- **Look for Deals:** Some budget hotels and hostels offer special deals, such as discounts for longer stays, free nights, or packages that include activities or meals. Be sure to check for any promotions when booking.

Making the Most of Your Budget Stay

Staying in budget accommodations in Lipari doesn't mean missing out on the island's charm and beauty. Many budget hotels, hostels, and guesthouses are run by locals who take pride in their hospitality and are eager to share the best of the island with their guests. By choosing budget-friendly options, you can stretch your travel funds further, allowing you to spend more on experiences, such as boat tours, local cuisine, and exploring the other Aeolian Islands.

With a wide range of affordable accommodations available, Lipari is an accessible destination for travelers of all budgets.

Camping and Alternative Stays in Lipari

For travelers looking to experience Lipari in a more immersive and unconventional way, camping and alternative stays offer a unique way to connect with nature and the local culture. It doesn't matter if you're a nature enthusiast who enjoys the simplicity of camping or an adventurous traveler seeking something different, Lipari has a variety of options that cater to these preferences.

Camping in Lipari

Camping in Lipari provides an opportunity to experience the island's natural beauty up close. While the island doesn't have many official campgrounds, the few that do exist offer a peaceful retreat where you can enjoy the stunning landscapes, clear skies, and the soothing sounds of the sea.

1. **Camping Baia Unci**
    - **Location:** Located in Canneto, just steps away from the beach, Camping Baia Unci is one of the few organized campsites on Lipari, offering a convenient base for beach lovers.
    - **Ambiance:** The campsite is surrounded by lush greenery, providing a tranquil environment for campers. You can pitch your tent under the shade of olive and pine trees, with the sound of waves lapping at the shore in the background.
    - **Facilities:** Baia Unci offers essential facilities such as restrooms, showers, a communal kitchen, and a small market. There are also shaded picnic areas where you can enjoy meals with fellow campers. The beach is just a short walk away, making it easy to take a dip in the sea whenever you please.
    - **Activities:** The campsite offers various activities, including snorkeling, kayaking, and boat tours. The friendly staff can also help arrange excursions to nearby islands or provide recommendations for hiking trails.
2. **Wild Camping**
    - **Location:** While wild camping is technically not permitted on Lipari, some adventurous travelers

choose to camp in more remote areas. If you do decide to go this route, it's essential to be respectful of the environment and follow the principles of Leave No Trace.
- **Ambiance:** Wild camping offers a more rugged and solitary experience, allowing you to immerse yourself fully in Lipari's natural landscapes. Whether you set up camp near the coast or in the island's interior hills, you'll be surrounded by breathtaking views and serenity.
- **Considerations:** Since wild camping is not officially sanctioned, it's important to be discreet and avoid setting up camp in populated or protected areas. Always carry out all trash, avoid lighting fires, and camp only for a night or two in one location to minimize your impact on the environment.

Alternative Stays: Unique Accommodations for a Memorable Experience

In addition to traditional hotels and guesthouses, Lipari offers a variety of alternative accommodations that provide a unique and memorable stay. These options range from eco-lodges to restored historic buildings, each offering a distinctive way to experience the island.

1. **Eco-Lodges**
   - **Location:** Several eco-lodges are scattered across Lipari, often located in more secluded and natural settings. These accommodations are designed to

minimize environmental impact while providing a comfortable and sustainable stay.
- **Ambiance:** Eco-lodges in Lipari are typically built using local, sustainable materials and are designed to blend harmoniously with the surrounding landscape. The decor is often rustic and natural, with an emphasis on comfort and simplicity. Staying at an eco-lodge allows you to connect with nature while enjoying modern amenities like solar-powered electricity and rainwater harvesting systems.
- **Activities:** Many eco-lodges offer guided nature walks, organic gardening experiences, and workshops on sustainable living. Some even have small farms where guests can participate in daily activities like harvesting vegetables or tending to animals.

2. **Agriturismo Stays**
   - **Location:** Agriturismo accommodations are found in the rural parts of Lipari, often on working farms or vineyards. These stays offer a glimpse into the island's agricultural traditions and provide a peaceful retreat from the more touristy areas.
   - **Ambiance:** Agriturismos typically offer a blend of rustic charm and modern comfort. Rooms or cottages are often housed in restored farm buildings, with decor that reflects the island's agricultural heritage. Guests can enjoy the tranquility of the countryside, with stunning views of vineyards, olive groves, and the sea.

- **Activities:** Guests staying at an agriturismo can often participate in farm activities, such as olive picking, wine tasting, or cooking classes featuring farm-fresh ingredients. Many agriturismos also offer guided tours of the property, where you can learn about sustainable farming practices and the island's agricultural history.

3. **Historical and Cultural Stays**
   - **Location:** For those interested in history and culture, Lipari offers accommodations in restored historical buildings, such as former monasteries, old villas, and traditional Aeolian houses. These stays provide a unique opportunity to experience the island's rich cultural heritage.
   - **Ambiance:** Staying in a historical property allows you to step back in time while enjoying modern comforts. Many of these properties retain their original architecture and features, such as stone walls, vaulted ceilings, and antique furnishings. The ambiance is often one of quiet elegance and timeless beauty.
   - **Activities:** Historical stays often include cultural activities, such as guided tours of the property, lectures on the island's history, and access to private gardens or chapels. Some properties also offer art or music workshops, allowing guests to engage with the island's cultural traditions in a hands-on way.

4. **Vacation Rentals**
   - **Location:** Vacation rentals are available throughout Lipari, from the bustling town center to more

remote villages. These accommodations range from apartments and villas to traditional Aeolian houses, offering a home-away-from-home experience.
- **Ambiance:** Vacation rentals provide the flexibility to create your own experience, with the comfort and convenience of a private space. Whether you choose a modern apartment in Lipari Town or a rustic villa in the countryside, you'll have the freedom to cook your meals, relax in private gardens or terraces, and explore the island at your own pace.
- **Activities:** Staying in a vacation rental allows you to live like a local, shopping at markets, preparing meals with fresh local ingredients, and exploring the island on your own terms. Many rentals are managed by local hosts who can provide insider tips and recommendations for your stay.

Considerations for Camping and Alternative Stays

- **Respect for Nature:** Whether you're camping or staying in an eco-lodge, it's essential to respect the environment. Follow the principles of Leave No Trace, conserve water and energy, and minimize your impact on the natural surroundings.
- **Booking in Advance:** Alternative accommodations, especially eco-lodges and agriturismos, often have limited availability, so it's advisable to book well in advance, particularly during peak tourist season.
- **Know the Rules:** If you plan to camp, make sure you're aware of the local regulations and restrictions. Some areas may have specific rules about where you can set up camp or what activities are permitted.

- **Prepare for the Weather:** Camping in Lipari means being exposed to the elements, so it's essential to be prepared. Bring appropriate gear for both hot and cooler temperatures, as well as protection from the sun and wind.

Making the Most of Your Alternative Stay

Staying in alternative accommodations on Lipari allows you to experience the island in a unique and meaningful way. Whether you're sleeping under the stars, immersing yourself in nature at an eco-lodge, or enjoying the rustic charm of a farmhouse, these options offer a deeper connection to the island's natural and cultural heritage. By choosing alternative stays, you'll not only enjoy a memorable experience but also support sustainable tourism and local communities.

Booking Platforms

Here's a list of useful websites and apps for finding accommodation options in Lipari, one of the Aeolian Islands off the coast of Sicily, Italy:

- **Booking.com**
    - **Features**: Offers a wide range of accommodation options on Lipari, including hotels, guesthouses, B&Bs, and vacation homes. Provides user reviews, photos, and detailed descriptions.
- **Airbnb**
    - **Features**: Ideal for finding unique stays such as private homes, villas, or apartments. Offers detailed property listings, host profiles, and user reviews.
    - **App**: Available on both iOS and Android.
- **Expedia**

- - **Features**: Provides a variety of lodging options, including hotels and vacation rentals. Often includes package deals with flights or car rentals.
- **Agoda**
  - **Features**: Known for competitive prices and a broad range of accommodations, from luxury stays to budget options. Includes reviews and photos.

2. Local and Specialty Platforms

- **Vrbo**
  - **Features**: Focuses on vacation rentals such as homes, villas, and apartments. Offers detailed property descriptions, photos, and user reviews.
- **ItalyXP**
  - **Features**: A travel platform dedicated to Italy, offering curated experiences and accommodation options in Lipari and other parts of the country.
- **HomeAway**
  - **Features**: Specializes in vacation rentals, offering a range of options from private homes to apartments on Lipari. Detailed property descriptions and user reviews are available.

3. Apps for Last-Minute Bookings

- **HotelTonight**
  - **Features**: Ideal for last-minute hotel deals. It offers exclusive discounts and a curated selection of hotels.
  - **App**: Available on both iOS and Android.

4. Comprehensive Travel Apps

- **TripAdvisor**

- **Features**: Offers a wide range of accommodation options along with user reviews, ratings, and traveler photos. Also provides insights into local attractions and restaurants.
    - **App**: Available on both iOS and Android.
- **Trivago**
    - **Features**: Compares prices from various booking sites to find the best deals on hotels and accommodations. Ideal for getting an overview of price options.

MUST-SEE ATTRACTIONS IN LIPARI: HIGHLIGHTS OF THE ISLAND

Lipari is rich with captivating attractions that draw visitors from all over the world. From ancient ruins to breathtaking natural wonders, the island offers a wide array of sights that are sure to enchant any traveler.

Lipari Castle

Lipari Castle, also known as Castello di Lipari, is one of the most significant historical landmarks on the island of Lipari. Its strategic position atop a steep promontory overlooking the town and harbor has made it a focal point of defense and power throughout the island's turbulent history. The site has been inhabited since the Neolithic period, but the castle itself has seen many transformations, with contributions from the Greeks, Romans, Byzantines, Normans, and Spanish, each leaving their mark on the fortress.

1. **Ancient Foundations**
    - **Prehistoric Settlement:** Archaeological evidence suggests that the area around Lipari Castle was first settled during the Neolithic period. The natural defenses provided by the steep cliffs made it an ideal location for early inhabitants to build their homes.
    - **Greek and Roman Era:** The Greeks fortified the site around the 4th century BC, constructing walls to protect the settlement from invaders. These fortifications were later expanded and reinforced during the Roman period, with additional structures

being added to accommodate the needs of the growing population.
2. **Medieval and Renaissance Developments**
    - **Byzantine and Norman Influence:** After the fall of the Western Roman Empire, the site fell under Byzantine control. The Byzantines built a new fortress on the ruins of the ancient acropolis. Later, the Normans captured the island in the 11th century and further strengthened the castle, using it as a base to control the surrounding seas.
    - **Spanish Era:** In the 16th century, under Spanish rule, the castle underwent significant reconstruction. The threat of pirate raids prompted the Spanish to fortify the walls further and add new defensive structures, including bastions and towers. The castle's imposing appearance today largely reflects these modifications.
3. **Modern Times**
    - **Decline and Restoration:** Over the centuries, the military importance of Lipari Castle declined, and parts of the structure fell into disrepair. However, in the 20th century, efforts were made to restore the castle and preserve its historical significance. Today, it stands as a testament to the island's rich and varied past, offering visitors a glimpse into the history of the Aeolian Islands.

Visitor Information

Lipari Castle is not only a historical landmark but also a cultural hub, housing several museums and offering breathtaking views of the surrounding area. Here's everything you need to know for a visit to this fascinating site.

1. **Getting There**
   - **Location:** The castle is located in the heart of Lipari Town, on a promontory that rises dramatically above the town and harbor. It is easily accessible on foot from most parts of the town.
   - **Access:** Visitors can reach the castle by walking up a series of steps and paths that wind their way up the hillside. The ascent is moderately steep, but the views along the way make it worthwhile. For those with mobility issues, taxis or rental cars can bring you close to the entrance, but the final approach must be done on foot.
2. **What to See**
   - **Aeolian Archaeological Museum:** One of the main attractions within the castle complex is the Aeolian Archaeological Museum, which houses an extensive collection of artifacts from the island's long history. The museum is divided into several sections, each focusing on different periods, from prehistoric times to the Roman era. Highlights include ancient pottery, tools, and a collection of well-preserved amphorae.
   - **The Ancient Walls and Towers:** As you explore the castle grounds, you'll come across the ancient walls and towers that once served as the island's primary defense. These structures offer a glimpse into the military architecture of different periods and provide stunning panoramic views of the

surrounding landscape, including the town of Lipari, the harbor, and the nearby islands.
- **The Cathedral of San Bartolomeo:** Within the castle complex, you'll also find the Cathedral of San Bartolomeo, dedicated to the patron saint of the Aeolian Islands. The cathedral, which dates back to the Norman period, features a beautiful baroque facade and an ornate interior. The cathedral is an important religious site and hosts various festivals and ceremonies throughout the year.

3. **Practical Information**
   - **Opening Hours:** The castle and its museums are generally open daily, with hours varying depending on the season. During the summer months, the castle may stay open later to accommodate the influx of tourists. It is recommended to check the current opening hours before planning your visit.
   - **Entry Fees:** There is an entry fee to visit the castle and the Aeolian Archaeological Museum. Tickets can be purchased at the entrance, and discounts are often available for students, seniors, and groups. Some sections of the castle may have separate admission fees, so be sure to inquire about any combined ticket options that may save you money.
   - **Guided Tours:** Guided tours are available and can provide a more in-depth understanding of the castle's history and significance. Tours are often available in multiple languages and can be arranged in advance or on the day of your visit. Audio guides are also available for those who prefer to explore at their own pace.

4. **Tips for Visitors**
    - **Wear Comfortable Shoes:** The castle grounds are expansive, and there is a fair amount of walking involved, often on uneven surfaces. Comfortable, sturdy footwear is recommended.
    - **Bring a Camera:** The castle offers some of the best views on the island, so be sure to bring a camera to capture the stunning scenery. The views from the castle walls, especially at sunset, are particularly breathtaking.
    - **Stay Hydrated:** If you're visiting during the warmer months, it's important to stay hydrated. There are a few cafes and shops near the entrance where you can purchase water and snacks before beginning your exploration.
    - **Plan for Extra Time:** The castle is a place where history enthusiasts could easily spend several hours, so plan your visit accordingly. If you're interested in visiting the museum and exploring all areas of the castle, allow at least half a day to fully experience everything.

Visiting Lipari Castle is like stepping back in time, where every corner reveals a piece of the island's rich history. Whether you're interested in ancient civilizations, military history, or simply enjoying breathtaking views, the castle offers something for every traveler. It's a must-visit destination on Lipari, providing both educational insights and unforgettable experiences.

Museo Archeologico Regionale Eoliano

The Museo Archeologico Regionale Eoliano, also known as the Aeolian Archaeological Museum, is one of the most important cultural and historical institutions in the Aeolian Islands. Located within the ancient walls of Lipari Castle, this museum offers visitors a fascinating journey through the rich history of the Aeolian Islands, showcasing artifacts that span thousands of years. From prehistoric tools to Roman-era relics, the museum's extensive collection provides a deep understanding of the islands' cultural heritage.

The Museum's Layout and Sections

The Aeolian Archaeological Museum is divided into several sections, each dedicated to a different period or aspect of the islands' history. As you explore the museum, you'll move through various galleries that highlight the most significant archaeological discoveries in the region.

1. **Prehistoric Section**
    - **Overview:** This section of the museum focuses on the early inhabitants of the Aeolian Islands, dating back to the Neolithic period. It offers insight into the lives of these early settlers, their tools, and their way of life.
    - **Highlights:** Expect to see stone tools, pottery, and artifacts that provide a glimpse into the daily activities and cultural practices of the island's first inhabitants. The displays also include burial sites and grave goods, shedding light on the spiritual beliefs of these ancient peoples.
2. **Bronze Age and Iron Age Section**

- **Overview:** This gallery delves into the Bronze Age and Iron Age periods, when the Aeolian Islands became an important hub for trade and cultural exchange in the Mediterranean.
- **Highlights:** Notable exhibits include beautifully crafted pottery, bronze tools, weapons, and ornaments. The section also features a reconstruction of a typical Bronze Age village, complete with models and diagrams that illustrate how the early inhabitants lived and interacted with their environment.

3. **Greek and Hellenistic Section**
    - **Overview:** The Greek and Hellenistic period was a time of great cultural development in the Aeolian Islands, with the islands playing a crucial role in the wider Greek world.
    - **Highlights:** This section boasts an impressive collection of Greek vases, amphorae, and sculptures. Among the most remarkable items are the terracotta theatrical masks, which were used in ancient Greek dramas and offer a unique insight into the island's cultural life during this period. Additionally, visitors can view artifacts from the necropolis, including elaborate grave goods that reflect the customs and beliefs of the time.

4. **Roman Section**
    - **Overview:** The Roman section showcases the influence of the Roman Empire on the Aeolian Islands, highlighting the transition from Greek to Roman rule.

- **Highlights:** Visitors can explore a wide range of Roman artifacts, including coins, glassware, and household items that reveal the everyday life of the Roman settlers on the islands. The museum also features remains of Roman villas and baths, which illustrate the luxury and sophistication of Roman architecture and engineering.

5. **Underwater Archaeology Section**
    - **Overview:** The waters surrounding the Aeolian Islands have been a rich source of archaeological discoveries, particularly shipwrecks that have yielded a treasure trove of artifacts.
    - **Highlights:** This section of the museum displays items recovered from the depths of the sea, including amphorae, anchors, and other maritime artifacts. These items tell the story of the islands' significance as a crossroads for ancient maritime trade routes. The section also includes detailed models and interactive displays that explain the techniques used in underwater archaeology.

6. **Volcanology Section**
    - **Overview:** The Aeolian Islands are of volcanic origin, and this section of the museum is dedicated to the study of volcanology and its impact on the islands' history and culture.
    - **Highlights:** Visitors can learn about the volcanic activity that shaped the islands, with displays featuring volcanic rocks, minerals, and even samples of volcanic ash. The section also includes informative panels that explain the science behind volcanic eruptions and their influence on the

development of the islands' landscape and human settlements.

Special Exhibits and Events

The Museo Archeologico Regionale Eoliano often hosts special exhibits and events that focus on specific themes or recent archaeological discoveries. These temporary exhibits provide a fresh perspective on the islands' history and offer visitors the chance to see rare and newly uncovered artifacts. Additionally, the museum organizes lectures, workshops, and guided tours led by experts in archaeology and history, providing a deeper understanding of the exhibits.

Visitor Information

1. **Location and Access**
   - **Address:** The museum is located within the Lipari Castle complex, a short walk from the center of Lipari Town. The entrance to the museum is clearly signposted within the castle grounds.
   - **How to Get There:** The museum is easily accessible on foot from most parts of Lipari Town. Visitors can also reach the castle by taxi or rental car, but the final approach to the museum requires a short walk.
2. **Opening Hours**
   - **General Hours:** The museum is typically open daily, with hours varying depending on the season. During the peak tourist season, the museum may extend its hours to accommodate more visitors. It is advisable to check the current opening hours on the

museum's official website or at the tourist information center in Lipari Town.
- **Special Hours:** On certain holidays or during special events, the museum may have different operating hours. Visitors should check in advance if they plan to visit during a public holiday or festival.

3. **Admission Fees**
   - **Ticket Prices:** There is an admission fee to enter the museum, with tickets available for purchase at the entrance. Discounts are often available for students, seniors, and children. The museum may also offer combined tickets that include entry to other parts of the Lipari Castle complex.
   - **Free Days:** The museum occasionally offers free admission on certain days, such as national holidays or during special events. Check the museum's schedule for upcoming free days.

4. **Guided Tours**
   - **Availability:** Guided tours are available in multiple languages and can be booked in advance or on the day of your visit. These tours provide a more in-depth exploration of the museum's exhibits and are led by knowledgeable guides who can answer questions and share additional insights.
   - **Audio Guides:** For visitors who prefer to explore at their own pace, audio guides are available for rent at the entrance. These guides offer detailed commentary on the exhibits and are a great option for those who want a self-guided experience.

5. **Facilities**

- **Gift Shop:** The museum has a gift shop that offers a range of souvenirs, books, and replicas of artifacts. It's a great place to pick up a memento of your visit or a gift for someone interested in history and archaeology.
- **Café:** A small café is located near the museum entrance, where visitors can enjoy light refreshments before or after their visit. The café offers a selection of snacks, beverages, and local specialties.
- **Restrooms:** Restroom facilities are available within the museum and are accessible to all visitors.

6. **Tips for Visitors**
    - **Time Needed:** Plan to spend at least two to three hours exploring the museum, especially if you want to take your time viewing the exhibits and reading the informational panels.
    - **Photography:** Photography is generally allowed in the museum, but flash photography and the use of tripods may be restricted. Be sure to check the museum's photography policy before taking pictures.
    - **Interactive Displays:** Take advantage of the interactive displays and multimedia presentations throughout the museum. These are especially engaging for children and provide a more dynamic learning experience.
    - **Accessibility:** The museum is housed in a historic building, and while efforts have been made to accommodate visitors with disabilities, some areas may be challenging to access. If you have specific

accessibility needs, contact the museum in advance to inquire about available services.

Spiaggia di Canneto

Spiaggia di Canneto is one of Lipari's most popular beaches, renowned for its beautiful setting, crystal-clear waters, and welcoming atmosphere. Located just a short distance from Lipari Town, this beach is a favorite among locals and visitors alike, offering a perfect spot to relax, swim, and enjoy the natural beauty of the Aeolian Islands. Whether you're looking for a family-friendly beach, a quiet place to sunbathe, or a base for water sports, Spiaggia di Canneto has something to offer everyone.

Overview of Canneto Beach

Spiaggia di Canneto stretches along the eastern coast of Lipari, offering a long expanse of pebbly shore bordered by the stunning turquoise waters of the Tyrrhenian Sea. The beach is divided into several sections, each with its own unique charm and appeal.

1. **The Beach Layout**
    - **Northern Section:** The northern end of Canneto Beach is quieter and less crowded, making it an ideal spot for those seeking tranquility. Here, you'll find fewer beach clubs and more open space where you can lay down your towel and enjoy the sun in peace.
    - **Central Section:** The central part of Canneto Beach is the most developed, with a variety of amenities, including beach clubs, bars, and restaurants. This area is perfect for those who want easy access to

facilities and services while enjoying their time on the beach.
- **Southern Section:** The southern end of the beach is popular with families due to its calm waters and proximity to amenities. The shallow entry into the sea makes it a safe spot for children to play and swim.

2. **Beach Composition**
   - **Pebbly Shoreline:** Like many of the beaches in the Aeolian Islands, Spiaggia di Canneto features a pebbly shoreline rather than sand. The pebbles are smooth and comfortable to walk on, but beachgoers may want to bring water shoes for added comfort.
   - **Clear Waters:** The waters at Canneto Beach are exceptionally clear, with varying shades of blue and green that create a mesmerizing contrast against the white pebbles. The clarity of the water makes it an ideal location for snorkeling and exploring the underwater world.

Facilities and Amenities

Spiaggia di Canneto is well-equipped with facilities that cater to the needs of visitors, making it a convenient and comfortable destination for a day at the beach.

1. **Beach Clubs (Lidos)**
   - **Overview:** Several beach clubs, or lidos, are located along Canneto Beach, offering sunbeds, umbrellas, and other services for a fee. These clubs provide a more luxurious beach experience, with amenities such as changing rooms, showers, and Wi-Fi.

- **Services:** In addition to sunbeds and umbrellas, many lidos offer food and beverage service directly to your spot on the beach, so you can enjoy a refreshing drink or a light snack without leaving your chair. Some clubs also have small shops selling beach essentials, such as sunscreen, towels, and inflatable toys.

2. **Dining Options**
    - **Beachfront Restaurants:** The beach is lined with several beachfront restaurants and cafes where you can enjoy a meal with a view. These establishments offer a range of options, from fresh seafood and traditional Aeolian dishes to international cuisine and quick bites.
    - **Snack Bars:** For a quick snack or a cold drink, there are several snack bars located along the beach. These are great spots to grab a gelato, a panini, or a refreshing granita to cool off on a hot day.

3. **Water Sports and Activities**
    - **Snorkeling:** The clear waters of Canneto Beach make it an excellent spot for snorkeling. Equipment can be rented from nearby shops, and guided snorkeling tours are also available for those who want to explore the underwater life more extensively.
    - **Kayaking and Paddleboarding:** Kayaks and paddleboards can be rented from various points along the beach. These activities are a fun and active way to explore the coastline and enjoy the sea from a different perspective.

- **Boat Rentals and Excursions:** For those who want to venture further, boat rentals and organized excursions to nearby islands and secluded beaches are available. These trips offer a chance to see the stunning coastline of Lipari and the surrounding Aeolian Islands from the water.

4. **Accessibility**
   - **For Families:** Spiaggia di Canneto is family-friendly, with calm waters, shallow entry points, and plenty of amenities nearby. The southern section of the beach is particularly popular with families.
   - **For Disabled Visitors:** While the pebbly terrain can be challenging, some areas of the beach are equipped with facilities to assist disabled visitors. Beach clubs may offer services such as accessible sunbeds and walkways to make the beach more accessible to everyone.

Best Time to Visit

The best time to visit Spiaggia di Canneto is during the summer months, from June to September, when the weather is warm and the sea is calm. During this period, the beach is lively, with plenty of activities and events taking place. However, it can get crowded, especially in July and August, so arriving early in the day is recommended to secure a good spot.

For those who prefer a quieter experience, visiting in the shoulder seasons, such as late May or early October, can be ideal. The weather is still pleasant, and the water remains warm enough for swimming, but the crowds are smaller, and the beach is more peaceful.

Nearby Attractions

Spiaggia di Canneto is not only a destination in its own right but also serves as a gateway to other attractions in the area.

1. **Pumice Quarries**
    - **Overview:** Just north of Canneto Beach, you'll find the famous pumice quarries, which have played a significant role in the island's history and economy. The stark white cliffs created by the pumice extraction contrast beautifully with the deep blue of the sea.
    - **Visiting:** While the quarries are no longer in operation, they are a fascinating site to visit, and the area around them is great for swimming and snorkeling in the crystal-clear waters.
2. **Acquacalda Beach**
    - **Overview:** Further north of Canneto lies Acquacalda Beach, another beautiful pebbly beach that is quieter and less developed than Canneto. It's a great spot for those looking to escape the crowds and enjoy a more tranquil setting.
    - **Activities:** The waters here are equally clear, making it another excellent location for snorkeling and swimming. The beach offers stunning views of the surrounding islands, particularly at sunset.
3. **Lipari Town**
    - **Overview:** Just a short distance from Canneto Beach, Lipari Town offers a variety of attractions, including the historic Lipari Castle, the Aeolian Archaeological Museum, and a range of shops, restaurants, and bars.

- **Exploring:** After a day at the beach, taking a stroll through the charming streets of Lipari Town is a great way to end your day. The town's vibrant atmosphere and rich history make it a must-visit on any trip to Lipari.

Tips for Visitors

1. **Bring Water Shoes:** The pebbly shore can be hard on bare feet, so bringing water shoes is recommended for added comfort while walking along the beach and entering the water.
2. **Arrive Early:** During peak season, the beach can become quite crowded, so arriving early in the morning will help you secure a good spot and enjoy the beach before it gets too busy.
3. **Stay Hydrated:** The sun can be strong, especially during the summer months, so make sure to bring plenty of water and stay hydrated throughout the day.
4. **Respect the Environment:** Like all natural areas, it's important to respect the beach and its surroundings. Make sure to dispose of trash properly, avoid disturbing wildlife, and be mindful of your impact on the environment.

Quattrocchi Viewpoint

Quattrocchi Viewpoint is one of the most breathtaking and iconic spots on the island of Lipari. Renowned for its stunning panoramic views, this viewpoint offers visitors an unparalleled perspective of the Aeolian Islands' rugged landscapes and azure waters. The name "Quattrocchi," which translates to "Four Eyes" in Italian, hints at the four distinct scenic elements you can capture from this vantage point: towering cliffs, volcanic formations, the sparkling sea, and the neighboring island of Vulcano. For both amateur and professional photographers, Quattrocchi is a dream location, offering endless opportunities to capture the natural beauty of Lipari.

Panoramic Views from Quattrocchi

The Quattrocchi Viewpoint provides sweeping views that encapsulate the raw beauty of the Aeolian Islands. The landscape here is dramatic, with steep cliffs plunging into the sea, lush greenery, and the contrasting hues of the deep blue Mediterranean waters.

1. **View of the Faraglioni Rocks**
    - **Overview:** One of the most striking features visible from Quattrocchi is the view of the Faraglioni rocks. These towering sea stacks rise majestically from the water just off the coast of Lipari, creating a dramatic focal point in the seascape.
    - **Photography Tip:** To capture the grandeur of the Faraglioni, consider using a wide-angle lens to include the surrounding cliffs and sea. Early morning or late afternoon light will enhance the textures and shadows, adding depth to your photos.
2. **Panoramic View of Vulcano Island**
    - **Overview:** From Quattrocchi, you can also enjoy a stunning view of the island of Vulcano, with its smoldering volcanic crater often visible in the distance. The contrast between the green slopes of Lipari and the rugged, volcanic landscape of Vulcano creates a captivating scene.

- **Photography Tip:** To capture the essence of Vulcano, use a telephoto lens to zoom in on the crater, especially when it's emitting smoke or steam. Including the surrounding sea and sky in your composition will provide context and highlight the island's volcanic nature.

3. **Cliffs and Coastline of Lipari**
   - **Overview:** The viewpoint also offers a magnificent perspective of Lipari's dramatic coastline, characterized by steep cliffs that plunge into the sea. The rugged terrain, dotted with Mediterranean vegetation, adds to the wild beauty of the scene.
   - **Photography Tip:** The cliffs are best photographed in the soft light of early morning or late afternoon when the sun is low in the sky. This lighting will emphasize the contours of the cliffs and bring out the rich colors of the landscape. Consider using a polarizing filter to enhance the contrast between the sky and sea.

4. **Sunset Views**
   - **Overview:** Quattrocchi is a fantastic spot to watch the sunset, with the sun dipping below the horizon and casting a golden glow over the sea and surrounding islands. The changing colors of the sky create a spectacular backdrop for photography.
   - **Photography Tip:** For capturing sunsets, use a tripod to keep your camera steady during longer exposures. Experiment with different exposure settings to capture the rich colors and subtle details of the scene. Don't forget to include some

foreground elements, like the cliffs or vegetation, to add depth to your composition.

Getting to Quattrocchi Viewpoint

Quattrocchi Viewpoint is easily accessible from Lipari Town, making it a popular stop for visitors exploring the island.

1. **Location and Access**
    - **Distance from Lipari Town:** Quattrocchi is located about 4 kilometers southwest of Lipari Town. The drive takes around 10 minutes, or you can opt for a scenic walk that takes approximately 45 minutes.
    - **How to Get There:** The viewpoint can be reached by car, scooter, or even on foot for those who enjoy hiking. The road to Quattrocchi is well-marked, and there is a small parking area nearby for those arriving by vehicle.

2. **Hiking to the Viewpoint**
   - **Overview:** For those who prefer an active approach, hiking to Quattrocchi Viewpoint is a rewarding experience. The route offers beautiful views along the way, passing through vineyards and olive groves.
   - **Route Tips:** The hike is moderate in difficulty, with some steep sections, so be sure to wear comfortable shoes and bring plenty of water. The trail is well-maintained, but it's advisable to start early in the morning or late in the afternoon to avoid the heat of the day.
3. **Guided Tours**
   - **Overview:** If you prefer a guided experience, several local tour operators offer excursions to Quattrocchi Viewpoint. These tours often include transportation, a guided walk, and commentary on the natural and cultural history of the area.
   - **Benefits:** A guided tour can provide deeper insights into the geology and history of the Aeolian Islands, as well as tips on the best spots for photography. It's also a great way to meet other travelers and share the experience.

Photography Tips for Quattrocchi Viewpoint

Quattrocchi Viewpoint is a photographer's paradise, offering a variety of subjects and compositions. Here are some tips to help you make the most of your photography experience.

Best Time for Photography

- **Golden Hour:** The golden hour, shortly after sunrise or before sunset, is the ideal time for photography at Quattrocchi. The soft, warm light during this time creates beautiful shadows and enhances the colors of the landscape.
- **Blue Hour:** The blue hour, just before sunrise or after sunset, offers a different mood, with cooler tones and a more serene atmosphere. This is a great time to capture the calmness of the sea and the silhouette of the islands.

Nearby Attractions

After enjoying the views at Quattrocchi, consider exploring other attractions nearby.

1. **Valle Muria Beach**
   - **Overview:** Located just a short distance from Quattrocchi, Valle Muria Beach is one of Lipari's hidden gems. This secluded beach is framed by dramatic cliffs and offers a peaceful escape from the more crowded beaches on the island.
   - **Activities:** Spend some time swimming, sunbathing, or snorkeling in the clear waters. The beach is also a great spot for a quiet picnic with a view.
2. **Pianoconte Village**
   - **Overview:** The nearby village of Pianoconte is worth a visit for its traditional Aeolian charm. Wander through the narrow streets, visit local shops, and enjoy a meal at one of the village's cozy trattorias.

- **Cultural Experience:** Pianoconte is known for its vibrant festivals and local traditions, so check if any events are happening during your visit for a chance to experience authentic Aeolian culture.

3. **Hiking Trails**
   - **Overview:** The area around Quattrocchi is crisscrossed with hiking trails that offer stunning views of the island and the sea. Whether you're looking for a short walk or a more challenging hike, there are plenty of options to explore.
   - **Trail Tips:** Some trails lead to other viewpoints, beaches, or secluded spots where you can enjoy the natural beauty of Lipari away from the crowds.

Tips for Visiting Quattrocchi Viewpoint

1. **Best Time to Visit:** To avoid the heat and crowds, visit Quattrocchi early in the morning or late in the afternoon. These times also offer the best lighting for photography.
2. **What to Bring:** Bring a hat, sunscreen, and plenty of water, especially if you plan to hike or stay at the viewpoint for an extended period. A camera with a fully charged battery and extra memory cards is also essential.
3. **Respect the Environment:** Quattrocchi is a natural site, so it's important to respect the environment. Avoid leaving any trash behind, stay on designated paths, and refrain from disturbing the local wildlife.

Churches and Religious Sites in Lipari: San Bartolomeo and More

Lipari is known for its deep-rooted religious heritage. The island is home to several beautiful churches and religious sites that reflect its centuries-old Christian tradition. These sacred places, often perched on hilltops or nestled within historic towns, offer visitors a glimpse into the island's spiritual and cultural identity. Whether you are a devout pilgrim, a history enthusiast, or simply a curious traveler, exploring Lipari's religious sites provides a unique insight into the island's past and its enduring faith.

San Bartolomeo Cathedral

San Bartolomeo Cathedral, also known as the Cathedral of St. Bartholomew, is the most important religious site on the island of Lipari. Dedicated to St. Bartholomew the Apostle, the patron saint of the Aeolian Islands, this cathedral holds a central place in the hearts of the local people. The cathedral, located in the historic center of Lipari Town, is a symbol of the island's rich religious and cultural heritage. It is not only a place of worship but also a repository of art, history, and tradition.

1. **Historical Background**
   - **Origins:** The original church on this site dates back to the Norman period, around the 11th century. It was built on the ruins of an ancient Roman basilica, which itself was constructed over a pre-Christian temple.
   - **Architectural Evolution:** Over the centuries, the cathedral has undergone numerous renovations and expansions, reflecting the different architectural

styles that have influenced the island. The current structure, with its Baroque façade, was largely shaped during the 17th and 18th centuries after suffering damage from various invasions and natural disasters.

2. **Architectural Features**
    - **Exterior:** The façade of San Bartolomeo Cathedral is a striking example of Baroque architecture, with ornate decorations, intricate stonework, and towering columns that draw the eye upward. The central portal is adorned with statues of saints, including St. Bartholomew, who is depicted holding a knife, a reference to his martyrdom.
    - **Interior:** The interior of the cathedral is equally impressive, with a soaring nave, richly decorated chapels, and a beautiful wooden ceiling painted with scenes from the life of St. Bartholomew. The altar, made of marble and adorned with gold accents, is the focal point of the cathedral, and behind it stands a large painting of the Madonna and Child, a work of art that dates back to the 16th century.
3. **Relics and Treasures**
    - **Relic of St. Bartholomew:** The cathedral houses a precious relic of St. Bartholomew, a piece of his skin, which is displayed in a silver reliquary. This relic is the centerpiece of the island's religious celebrations, especially during the annual feast of St. Bartholomew in August.
    - **Artworks:** San Bartolomeo Cathedral is home to several significant works of religious art, including paintings, statues, and frescoes. Notable pieces include a 17th-century painting of the Last Supper and a statue of St. Bartholomew that is carried through the streets of Lipari during processions.

4. **Visiting the Cathedral**
    - **Opening Hours:** San Bartolomeo Cathedral is open to visitors throughout the year, with specific hours for worship and tours. It is advisable to check the opening times before your visit, especially during religious holidays and festivals.
    - **Guided Tours:** For those interested in the history and art of the cathedral, guided tours are available. These tours provide a deeper understanding of the site's significance and the stories behind its treasures.

Religious Significance and Festivities

San Bartolomeo Cathedral is the focal point of religious life in Lipari, particularly during the feast of St. Bartholomew, which is celebrated with great fervor. The feast, held annually on August 24th, includes religious processions, mass, and various cultural events. The highlight of the celebration is the procession of the statue of St. Bartholomew, carried through the streets of Lipari Town, accompanied by prayers, hymns, and the participation of the local community.

Other Notable Churches and Religious Sites in Lipari

Church of the Immaculate Conception

The Church of the Immaculate Conception, locally known as Chiesa dell'Immacolata, is another significant religious site in Lipari. Located near San Bartolomeo Cathedral, this church is part of the same religious complex and shares a rich history with it.

1. **Historical Background**

- **Origins:** The Church of the Immaculate Conception was originally built in the 12th century as part of a Benedictine monastery. It has since been renovated and expanded, with its current appearance dating back to the 18th century.
- **Architectural Style:** The church features a simple yet elegant façade with a modest bell tower. The interior, though less ornate than the cathedral, is notable for its serene atmosphere and the beautiful frescoes that adorn the walls and ceiling.

2. **Religious Art and Relics**
   - **Altar and Frescoes:** The main altar of the church is dedicated to the Immaculate Conception and features a statue of the Virgin Mary surrounded by angels. The frescoes, depicting scenes from the life of the Virgin Mary, are a highlight of the church's interior.
   - **Relics:** The church also houses relics of several saints, which are displayed during special religious ceremonies.
3. **Cultural Importance**
   - **Feast of the Immaculate Conception:** The church is the center of the island's celebrations on December 8th, the Feast of the Immaculate Conception. The day is marked by mass, processions, and community gatherings.

Church of San Giuseppe

The Church of San Giuseppe, dedicated to St. Joseph, is located in the area of Marina Corta, offering a beautiful view of the harbor and the sea. This church is one of Lipari's oldest religious buildings and holds a special place in the island's spiritual life.

1. **Architectural Overview**
   - **Facade and Interior:** The church features a simple and traditional façade, reflecting the modesty associated with St. Joseph. Inside, the church is adorned with a number of statues and paintings, including a notable depiction of St. Joseph holding the infant Jesus.
   - **Bell Tower:** The bell tower of the Church of San Giuseppe is a prominent feature, providing a picturesque backdrop to the Marina Corta area. The sound of its bells ringing out across the harbor is a familiar and comforting presence for locals and visitors alike.
2. **Religious Celebrations**
   - **Feast of St. Joseph:** The Church of San Giuseppe is the focal point for the Feast of St. Joseph, celebrated on March 19th. This day is marked by a special mass, followed by processions and communal meals. The feast is an important event in Lipari, reflecting the islanders' deep devotion to St. Joseph.

Church of San Pietro

The Church of San Pietro is another notable religious site in Lipari, located in the area of Marina Lunga. This church, dedicated to St. Peter, is known for its tranquil setting and the beautiful views it offers of the surrounding landscape.

1. **History and Architecture**
   - **Founding:** The Church of San Pietro was founded in the 16th century and has been an important place of worship for the fishing community of Lipari.
   - **Design:** The church's design is simple and unadorned, with a whitewashed exterior and a small bell tower. The interior is equally modest, with a few religious statues and paintings that reflect the church's maritime heritage.
2. **Maritime Connections**
   - **Blessing of the Boats:** The Church of San Pietro is closely associated with Lipari's fishing community. Every year, on the feast day of St. Peter (June 29th), a special ceremony is held to bless the boats in the harbor. This tradition, known as the Blessing of the Boats, is a deeply rooted custom in Lipari, reflecting the community's reliance on the sea for their livelihood.

Church of Santa Caterina

The Church of Santa Caterina, dedicated to St. Catherine of Alexandria, is located in the area of Pianoconte, a small village on the island of Lipari. This church is known for its peaceful atmosphere and its importance to the local community.

1. **Architectural Highlights**
   - **Simple Design:** The Church of Santa Caterina is a small, simple structure that reflects the rural character of Pianoconte. The church's white exterior and red-tiled roof blend harmoniously with the surrounding landscape.

- **Interior Features:** Inside, the church is adorned with a few religious artifacts, including a statue of St. Catherine and a painting of her martyrdom. The altar is modest but beautifully crafted, serving as the focal point of the church.

2. **Community Role**
   - **Local Celebrations:** The Church of Santa Caterina plays a central role in the religious life of Pianoconte. The feast of St. Catherine, celebrated on November 25th, is a significant event in the village, featuring mass, processions, and traditional meals shared by the community.

EXPLORING NATURE IN LIPARI

Lipari is a treasure trove for nature lovers, offering diverse landscapes and outdoor adventures. The island's natural beauty is showcased through its rugged cliffs, lush greenery, and pristine beaches, making it a paradise for hikers, beachgoers, and anyone looking to connect with the great outdoors.

Diverse Landscapes and Scenic Beauty

Lipari's landscape is a harmonious blend of volcanic mountains, verdant valleys, and azure seas. The island's volcanic origins have shaped its unique topography, creating a terrain that is both dramatic and inviting. As you explore Lipari, you'll encounter towering cliffs that plunge into the sea, fertile agricultural land dotted with vineyards, and secluded coves where the crystal-clear waters beckon.

1. **Volcanic Origins**
    - **Historical Impact:** Lipari's volcanic history is evident in its rugged terrain and black sand beaches. The island's geological past has created a landscape that is both striking and fertile, with rich soil that supports vineyards and orchards.
    - **Pumice Quarries:** One of the most fascinating features of Lipari's landscape is the pumice quarries, where gleaming white pumice stone has been extracted for centuries. These quarries, located on the northern coast, offer a surreal, almost lunar, landscape that is a must-see for visitors.

2. **Coastal Beauty**
    - **Stunning Cliffs:** The island's coastline is defined by steep cliffs that offer breathtaking views of the surrounding sea and neighboring islands. One of the best ways to experience these cliffs is by taking a boat tour around the island, where you can marvel at the dramatic rock formations and hidden caves.
    - **Beaches and Coves:** Lipari is home to some of the most beautiful beaches in the Aeolian Islands. Whether you prefer the black sand beaches of Canneto or the white pebble shores of Acquacalda, there's a beach for every type of traveler. Many of these beaches are accessible only by boat, adding to their secluded charm.

Hiking Trails and Scenic Walks in Lipari

Lipari, with its stunning landscapes and rich history, is a haven for hikers and nature lovers. The island's varied terrain, ranging from volcanic peaks to coastal cliffs, offers a diverse array of hiking trails and scenic walks that cater to all levels of fitness and experience. Whether you're an avid hiker looking for a challenging ascent or someone who prefers a leisurely stroll with breathtaking views, Lipari has something to offer.

Overview of Lipari's Hiking Experience

Hiking in Lipari is a journey through time and nature. The island's trails take you through ancient paths once trodden by the island's earliest inhabitants, past archaeological sites, and through landscapes shaped by volcanic activity. As you hike, you'll be treated to panoramic views of the Aeolian Islands, the shimmering Mediterranean Sea, and the lush, green interior of Lipari.

1. **Diverse Terrain**
    - **Volcanic Landscapes:** Lipari's volcanic origins are evident in its rugged terrain, with black sand beaches, pumice quarries, and jagged rock formations. Hiking through these areas offers a unique opportunity to witness the island's geological history up close.
    - **Coastal Cliffs:** The island's dramatic cliffs provide some of the most scenic walks, offering stunning views of the surrounding sea and neighboring islands. These coastal paths are perfect for those who want to enjoy the island's natural beauty without too much exertion.
    - **Lush Interiors:** Away from the coast, Lipari's interior is a verdant landscape of vineyards, olive groves, and forested hills. The island's rural paths lead you through this tranquil countryside, where you can enjoy the sights and sounds of nature.

Top Hiking Trails in Lipari

1. Monte Sant'Angelo Trail

The Monte Sant'Angelo Trail is one of the most popular hikes on Lipari, offering spectacular views and a challenging ascent.

- **Trail Overview:**
    - **Starting Point:** Lipari Town
    - **Distance:** Approximately 8 kilometers (round trip)
    - **Difficulty:** Moderate to Difficult
    - **Elevation Gain:** 594 meters

- **Trail Description:**
  - **The Ascent:** The hike begins in Lipari Town and quickly ascends through a series of switchbacks. As you climb, the views of the town and the harbor become increasingly impressive. The trail is well-marked, but the steepness of the ascent makes it a challenging hike, especially in the heat of summer.
  - **Panoramic Views:** Upon reaching the summit of Monte Sant'Angelo, you are rewarded with panoramic views of Lipari and the surrounding Aeolian Islands. On a clear day, you can see as far as Stromboli, Panarea, and even the coast of Sicily. The summit is a perfect spot to take a break, enjoy a picnic, and soak in the breathtaking scenery.
  - **Descent:** The descent follows the same route back to Lipari Town, offering a chance to revisit the stunning views and enjoy the changing light as the day progresses.

2. Quattrocchi Viewpoint Trail

The Quattrocchi Viewpoint Trail is a shorter, less strenuous hike that leads to one of the most famous viewpoints on the island.

- **Trail Overview:**
  - **Starting Point:** Pianoconte Village
  - **Distance:** Approximately 4 kilometers (round trip)
  - **Difficulty:** Easy to Moderate
- **Trail Description:**
  - **The Walk:** The trail begins in the village of Pianoconte and meanders through the countryside, passing vineyards, orchards, and traditional Aeolian

houses. The path is relatively flat, making it suitable for hikers of all ages and abilities.
- **Quattrocchi Viewpoint:** The highlight of this hike is the Quattrocchi Viewpoint, where you'll be treated to stunning views of the cliffs, the sea, and the neighboring island of Vulcano. The viewpoint is particularly popular at sunset when the light casts a golden glow over the landscape, creating a perfect photo opportunity.
- **Return:** After taking in the views, you can either return the way you came or continue along the trail to explore more of the surrounding countryside.

3. Monte Guardia Trail

For those seeking a less crowded trail with equally stunning views, the Monte Guardia Trail offers a peaceful and rewarding hike.

- **Trail Overview:**
    - **Starting Point:** Lipari Town or Pianoconte
    - **Distance:** Approximately 5 kilometers (round trip)
    - **Difficulty:** Moderate
- **Trail Description:**
    - **The Ascent:** The trail to Monte Guardia is less steep than Monte Sant'Angelo, but it still provides a good workout. The path winds through forests and open fields, offering glimpses of the sea and the surrounding islands as you climb.
    - **Summit Views:** At the summit of Monte Guardia, you'll find sweeping views of Lipari, the sea, and the other Aeolian Islands. This quieter spot is

perfect for those who prefer solitude and a more immersive experience in nature.
- **Wildlife and Flora:** The trail is also known for its rich biodiversity, with a variety of plants, birds, and butterflies to observe along the way.

4. Acquacalda to Porticello Coastal Walk

The Acquacalda to Porticello Coastal Walk is a scenic route that takes you along the northern coast of Lipari, offering beautiful coastal views and a glimpse into the island's pumice industry.

- **Trail Overview:**
    - **Starting Point:** Acquacalda Village
    - **Distance:** Approximately 6 kilometers (one way)
    - **Difficulty:** Easy to Moderate
- **Trail Description:**
    - **Coastal Path:** The trail follows the coastline from Acquacalda to the old pumice quarries at Porticello. Along the way, you'll pass by pebble beaches, cliffs, and the white pumice slopes that give the area a unique, almost otherworldly appearance.
    - **Pumice Quarries:** The trail offers a fascinating look at the island's pumice industry, which was once a major economic activity on Lipari. The abandoned quarries and factory buildings add an element of industrial history to the hike.
    - **Swimming Spots:** There are several spots along the trail where you can take a dip in the clear, blue waters of the Tyrrhenian Sea. These secluded coves are perfect for a refreshing swim or a relaxing break.

5. Lipari Archaeological Walk

For those interested in combining hiking with history, the Lipari Archaeological Walk offers a fascinating journey through the island's ancient past.

- **Trail Overview:**
    - **Starting Point:** Lipari Town
    - **Distance:** Varies depending on the route
    - **Difficulty:** Easy
- **Trail Description:**
    - **Historical Sites:** The walk takes you through Lipari Town and up to the archaeological park, where you can explore ancient Greek and Roman ruins, including the remnants of the city walls, a necropolis, and a Roman amphitheater.
    - **Cultural Insights:** Along the way, you'll also pass by several museums, including the Museo Archeologico Regionale Eoliano, where you can learn more about the island's rich history and cultural heritage.
    - **Relaxed Pace:** This walk is more of a leisurely exploration than a strenuous hike, making it ideal for those who want to combine a bit of exercise with a deep dive into the island's history.

Tips for Hiking in Lipari

- **Best Time to Hike:** The best time to hike in Lipari is during the spring (April to June) and fall (September to October) when the weather is mild, and the trails are less crowded. Summer can be hot, so if you're hiking during

this time, start early in the morning to avoid the midday heat.
- **What to Bring:** Always carry plenty of water, sunscreen, and a hat, as the sun can be intense, especially on exposed trails. Sturdy hiking shoes are recommended, as the terrain can be rocky and uneven.
- **Respect Nature:** Lipari's natural environment is fragile, so be sure to stay on marked trails, avoid disturbing wildlife, and carry out all trash.
- **Safety First:** Some trails, particularly those leading to higher elevations, can be challenging. Make sure you're in good physical condition and know your limits. If you're unsure about a trail, consider hiring a local guide.

Boat Tours and Island Hopping in Lipari

Lipari serves as a perfect gateway for exploring the surrounding archipelago through boat tours and island-hopping adventures. The island's strategic location in the Tyrrhenian Sea, coupled with its stunning coastline and nearby islets, makes it an ideal base for travelers eager to discover the beauty and diversity of the Aeolian Islands. Whether you're interested in exploring hidden coves, snorkeling in crystal-clear waters, or visiting other volcanic islands, Lipari's boat tours and island-hopping excursions offer an unforgettable way to experience the region.

Overview of Boat Tours in Lipari

Boat tours from Lipari provide a unique perspective of the island's dramatic coastline and offer easy access to the neighboring Aeolian Islands. These tours are perfect for travelers who want to explore multiple destinations in a single day, enjoy the serenity of the open sea, and discover secluded spots that are often inaccessible by land.

1. **Types of Boat Tours**
   - **Day Trips:** These are full-day excursions that typically include visits to one or more of the neighboring islands, with stops for swimming, snorkeling, and exploring.
   - **Half-Day Tours:** Ideal for those with limited time, half-day tours focus on specific areas around Lipari, such as the northern or southern coast, and may include a visit to a nearby island like Vulcano or Panarea.
   - **Sunset Cruises:** For a romantic experience, sunset cruises offer a leisurely sail around the island, with stunning views of the sun setting over the sea.
   - **Private Charters:** For a more personalized experience, private boat charters allow you to customize your itinerary and explore the islands at your own pace.

2. **What to Expect on a Boat Tour**
   - **Scenic Views:** Boat tours offer unparalleled views of Lipari's cliffs, beaches, and rock formations. As you sail around the island, you'll be able to see the dramatic landscape from a completely different angle, with opportunities to photograph iconic landmarks like the Faraglioni rocks and the pumice quarries.
   - **Swimming and Snorkeling:** Many boat tours include stops at secluded coves and bays where you can swim in the turquoise waters or snorkel to explore the vibrant marine life. Popular spots include the Grotta del Cavallo and the beaches of Canneto and Acquacalda.

- **Cultural and Historical Insights:** Some boat tours include guided commentary on the history and culture of the Aeolian Islands, providing interesting facts about the region's volcanic origins, ancient settlements, and maritime heritage.
- **Local Cuisine:** Depending on the tour, you may be treated to a meal or snack onboard, featuring local specialties like fresh seafood, Aeolian capers, and Malvasia wine.

Popular Island-Hopping Destinations from Lipari

Island hopping from Lipari allows you to explore the diverse landscapes, unique cultures, and varied attractions of the Aeolian Islands. Each island has its own distinct character and appeal, making island hopping a rich and rewarding experience.

1. Vulcano

Vulcano, the closest island to Lipari, is famous for its active volcano, therapeutic mud baths, and dramatic landscapes.

- **Highlights:**
    - **Gran Cratere:** The island's most iconic feature is the Gran Cratere, an active volcanic crater that can be reached by a moderately challenging hike. From the summit, you'll have panoramic views of the entire Aeolian archipelago.
    - **Mud Baths and Hot Springs:** Vulcano is known for its natural mud baths and hot springs, which are believed to have therapeutic properties. After a day of exploring, relax in the warm, mineral-rich waters.

- **Beaches:** The island's black sand beaches, such as Spiaggia delle Sabbie Nere, are perfect for sunbathing and swimming.
- **Boat Tours:**
  - **Day Trip to Vulcano:** Many boat tours from Lipari include a stop at Vulcano, allowing you to hike to the crater, enjoy the mud baths, and explore the island's beaches.

2. Salina

Salina, the second-largest island in the archipelago, is known for its lush landscapes, vineyards, and charming villages.

- **Highlights:**
  - **Monte Fossa delle Felci:** The island's highest peak offers challenging hiking trails with rewarding views of the Aeolian Islands and the Sicilian coast.
  - **Malfa and Santa Marina:** These picturesque villages are known for their colorful houses, quaint streets, and excellent local restaurants.
  - **Wineries:** Salina is famous for its Malvasia wine, a sweet dessert wine produced from grapes grown on the island's fertile slopes. Visiting a local winery for a tasting is a must-do activity.
- **Boat Tours:**
  - **Day Trip to Salina:** A day trip to Salina typically includes a visit to the island's main villages, a stop at the Pollara beach (famous for its appearance in the film "Il Postino"), and opportunities for swimming and wine tasting.

3. Panarea

Panarea, the smallest and most exclusive of the Aeolian Islands, is a favorite among celebrities and offers a chic, upscale vibe.

- **Highlights:**
    - **Whitewashed Houses and Boutiques:** The island's charming town is known for its whitewashed houses, boutique shops, and trendy restaurants.
    - **Cala Junco:** This stunning bay is one of the most beautiful swimming spots in the Aeolian Islands, with clear waters and a rocky beach.
    - **Prehistoric Village:** Panarea is home to a well-preserved prehistoric village, where you can explore ancient ruins dating back to the Bronze Age.
- **Boat Tours:**
    - **Panarea and Stromboli by Night:** A popular boat tour combines a visit to Panarea with an evening trip to Stromboli, where you can witness the island's active volcano erupting against the night sky.

4. Stromboli

Stromboli, known as the "Lighthouse of the Mediterranean," is famous for its constantly active volcano and dramatic eruptions.

- **Highlights:**
    - **Sciara del Fuoco:** The island's most spectacular feature is the Sciara del Fuoco, a steep slope where lava flows into the sea. Watching the eruptions from a boat at night is a once-in-a-lifetime experience.

- - **Ginostra:** This tiny village, accessible only by boat, offers a glimpse into traditional island life and is a peaceful escape from the more touristy areas.
  - **Volcano Hikes:** For the adventurous, guided hikes to the summit of Stromboli are available, offering close-up views of the volcanic activity.
- **Boat Tours:**
  - **Stromboli by Night:** One of the most popular tours from Lipari, this evening excursion takes you to Stromboli, where you can watch the volcano's eruptions from the safety of a boat offshore.

5. Filicudi and Alicudi

Filicudi and Alicudi, the most remote of the Aeolian Islands, are perfect for those seeking tranquility and unspoiled nature.

- **Highlights:**
  - **Untouched Nature:** Both islands are known for their rugged landscapes, crystal-clear waters, and traditional way of life. They offer a true escape from the hustle and bustle of modern life.
  - **Hiking Trails:** Filicudi has several scenic hiking trails, including one to the ancient village of Zucco Grande, while Alicudi offers challenging walks up its steep, terraced hillsides.
  - **Marine Life:** The waters around Filicudi and Alicudi are teeming with marine life, making them ideal for snorkeling and diving.
- **Boat Tours:**
  - **Day Trip to Filicudi and Alicudi:** These islands are often included in longer, full-day boat tours

from Lipari, with stops for swimming, snorkeling, and exploring the local villages.

Practical Tips for Boat Tours and Island Hopping

- **Booking:** Boat tours can be booked in advance online or in person at the harbor in Lipari Town. It's advisable to book early, especially during the peak summer season.
- **What to Bring:** Essentials for a boat tour include sunscreen, a hat, sunglasses, swimwear, a towel, and a camera. Don't forget to bring water and snacks, although many tours provide refreshments.
- **Weather Considerations:** The weather can change quickly on the sea, so it's important to check the forecast and be prepared for wind and waves. Tours may be canceled or rescheduled in case of bad weather.
- **Comfort:** If you're prone to seasickness, consider taking medication before setting off. Comfortable, non-slip footwear is also recommended for moving around the boat.

Snorkeling and Diving Spots in Lipari

The island of Lipari is surrounded by the pristine waters of the Tyrrhenian Sea, making it a paradise for snorkeling and diving enthusiasts. With its volcanic origins, Lipari offers a unique underwater landscape filled with rich marine life, fascinating geological formations, and historical shipwrecks. If you're a seasoned diver or a beginner snorkeler, Lipari's coastal waters provide an unforgettable experience beneath the waves.

Overview of Snorkeling and Diving in Lipari

Lipari's underwater world is characterized by crystal-clear waters, excellent visibility, and diverse marine habitats. The island's volcanic history has created a dramatic seascape of underwater cliffs, caves, and canyons, alongside soft, sandy bottoms that are home to a variety of sea creatures. The relatively mild water temperatures and calm conditions make snorkeling and diving accessible year-round, though the best time to explore is from late spring to early autumn.

1. **Marine Life**
    - **Fish Species:** The waters around Lipari are teeming with colorful fish, including groupers, sea bream, damselfish, and the occasional barracuda. In shallower areas, you might encounter schools of sardines and mackerel, while deeper waters reveal larger species and pelagic fish.
    - **Invertebrates and Corals:** Sponges, sea anemones, and vibrant coral formations add color to the underwater landscape. You'll also find an abundance of octopuses, starfish, and sea urchins hiding among the rocks.
    - **Nudibranchs and Other Critters:** Lipari is a haven for macro enthusiasts, with an array of nudibranchs (sea slugs), crustaceans, and other small creatures that thrive in the nutrient-rich waters.

2. **Underwater Landscapes**
    - **Volcanic Formations:** The volcanic activity that shaped Lipari above the surface also created a fascinating underwater environment. Divers and

snorkelers can explore lava flows, submerged craters, and black sand bottoms that tell the story of the island's fiery past.

- **Caves and Grottos:** Lipari's coastline is dotted with caves and grottos, many of which extend below the waterline. These underwater caves provide a thrilling environment for divers, with opportunities to explore hidden chambers and discover marine life that prefers the darkness of these sheltered spaces.

- **Shipwrecks:** For history buffs, Lipari offers several dive sites with ancient shipwrecks, including Roman and Greek vessels that have been preserved in the island's waters for centuries. These sites offer a glimpse into the maritime history of the region and are home to a variety of marine life that has made these wrecks their habitat.

Top Snorkeling and Diving Spots in Lipari

1. Pietra del Bagno

Pietra del Bagno is one of the most popular snorkeling spots on Lipari, known for its clear waters and abundant marine life.

- **Location:** Located on the western coast of Lipari, near the village of Quattropani.
- **What to Expect:** The shallow, calm waters make Pietra del Bagno an ideal spot for beginners and families. The area is home to colorful fish, octopuses, and occasionally, the shy moray eel. The rocky seabed provides a great environment for snorkeling, with plenty of nooks and crannies to explore.

- **Highlights:** The highlight of this spot is the large rock formations that rise from the sea, providing both a visual spectacle and a habitat for a diverse range of marine species.

2. Grotta del Cavallo

Grotta del Cavallo, or "Cave of the Horse," is a must-visit site for both snorkelers and divers, offering a mix of adventure and beauty.

- **Location:** Situated on the southern coast of Lipari, near the town of Canneto.
- **What to Expect:** The grotto is accessible by boat, and snorkelers can explore the entrance and the surrounding waters, where sunlight filters through, creating a magical underwater environment. For divers, the cave extends deeper into the rock, revealing a labyrinth of tunnels and chambers.
- **Highlights:** Inside the grotto, you'll find impressive stalactites and stalagmites, along with schools of fish that dart in and out of the shadows. The play of light and color in this underwater cave makes it a photographer's dream.

3. Secca di Capistello

Secca di Capistello is one of Lipari's premier diving sites, known for its stunning underwater topography and rich biodiversity.

- **Location:** Off the southeastern coast of Lipari, near the village of Capistello.
- **What to Expect:** This dive site features a series of underwater pinnacles that rise from the seabed, creating a dramatic seascape. The area is teeming with marine life,

including groupers, amberjacks, and barracudas. The pinnacles are covered in sponges and corals, providing a colorful backdrop for your dive.
- **Highlights:** The highlight of Secca di Capistello is the chance to spot larger pelagic species, as well as the diverse array of smaller fish that inhabit the coral-covered rocks. The site is suitable for intermediate to advanced divers due to its depth and occasional currents.

4. Porticello Beach

Porticello Beach, located on the northern coast of Lipari, offers a combination of beach relaxation and excellent snorkeling opportunities.

- **Location:** Northern coast, near the pumice quarries of Porticello.
- **What to Expect:** The waters here are shallow and clear, with a sandy bottom that gradually slopes into deeper water. The area is known for its pumice stone formations, which create an interesting underwater landscape. Snorkelers can expect to see a variety of small fish, as well as the occasional octopus or cuttlefish.
- **Highlights:** The contrast between the white pumice stones and the deep blue water makes for a visually striking environment. The area is also relatively uncrowded, offering a peaceful snorkeling experience.

5. Punta Castagna

Punta Castagna is another top diving spot in Lipari, renowned for its volcanic formations and vibrant marine life.

- **Location:** Located on the eastern coast of Lipari, near the village of Acquacalda.
- **What to Expect:** The site features a dramatic underwater landscape of volcanic rocks and cliffs, with plenty of crevices and overhangs to explore. Divers will find an abundance of fish, including groupers, wrasses, and damselfish, as well as octopuses and crustaceans hiding among the rocks.
- **Highlights:** The unique volcanic features, combined with the rich marine life, make Punta Castagna a favorite among divers. The site's depth and the potential for strong currents mean it's best suited for experienced divers.

Diving Centers and Snorkeling Tours

For those new to snorkeling or diving, Lipari offers several diving centers and guided tours that provide everything you need for a safe and enjoyable experience.

1. **Diving Centers:**
   - **PADI Certified:** Most diving centers in Lipari are PADI certified, offering courses for beginners, advanced divers, and specialty dives like night diving or wreck diving.
   - **Equipment Rental:** These centers provide full equipment rental, including wetsuits, fins, masks, and tanks, ensuring you have everything you need for your underwater adventure.
2. **Snorkeling Tours:**
   - **Guided Snorkeling Trips:** If you prefer a guided experience, snorkeling tours are available that take

you to the best spots around the island. These tours often include boat transportation, snorkeling gear, and a knowledgeable guide who can point out interesting marine life and ensure your safety.
- **Private Charters:** For a more personalized experience, consider booking a private charter that allows you to explore multiple snorkeling spots at your own pace.

Practical Tips for Snorkeling and Diving in Lipari

- **Best Time to Go:** The best time for snorkeling and diving in Lipari is from May to October, when the water is warmest, and visibility is at its best. During these months, the sea is generally calm, making conditions ideal for underwater exploration.
- **Safety First:** Always prioritize safety when snorkeling or diving. Make sure you're familiar with your equipment, never dive or snorkel alone, and be aware of your surroundings. If you're diving, adhere to your training and dive within your limits.
- **Environmental Responsibility:** Lipari's underwater ecosystems are fragile, so it's important to practice responsible snorkeling and diving. Avoid touching or disturbing marine life, don't collect any souvenirs from the sea, and be mindful of your fins to avoid damaging coral or stirring up sediment.
- **What to Bring:** For snorkeling, bring a mask, snorkel, fins, and a wetsuit if the water is chilly. Divers should ensure they have all necessary gear or rent it from a reputable dive shop. Sunscreen is also important, but choose a reef-safe variety to protect the marine environment.

Nature Reserves and Protected Areas in Lipari

Lipari, the largest of the Aeolian Islands, is not just a treasure trove of history and culture but also a haven for nature enthusiasts. The island's diverse landscapes, shaped by volcanic activity, are dotted with unique flora and fauna, offering numerous opportunities to explore and connect with the natural environment. Lipari's nature reserves and protected areas are vital for preserving its ecological heritage, providing visitors with a chance to experience the island's unspoiled beauty.

Overview of Nature Reserves and Protected Areas

Lipari's natural environment is protected through a network of reserves and conservation areas, designed to safeguard the island's unique ecosystems. These areas include coastal and marine environments, as well as inland reserves that encompass the island's diverse volcanic landscape. The protection of these areas ensures the preservation of Lipari's native species, some of which are endemic to the Aeolian Islands, and helps maintain the island's ecological balance.

1. **Flora and Fauna:**
    - **Flora:** Lipari's vegetation is characterized by Mediterranean scrub, including species such as juniper, rosemary, and wild thyme. In the more fertile areas, you can find olive groves, vineyards, and citrus orchards. The island's volcanic soils also support a range of rare plants, including some that are unique to the Aeolian archipelago.
    - **Fauna:** The island is home to a variety of wildlife, including reptiles like the Aeolian wall lizard, birds such as peregrine falcons and hoopoes, and marine

life in the surrounding waters, including dolphins, sea turtles, and a diverse array of fish species.

2. **Volcanic Landscapes:**
    - **Lava Fields and Craters:** The island's volcanic heritage is evident in its rugged terrain, with ancient lava flows, craters, and pumice quarries shaping the landscape. These geological features are not only visually striking but also provide unique habitats for specialized plant and animal species.
    - **Cliffs and Coastal Formations:** Lipari's coastline is marked by dramatic cliffs and rocky outcrops, offering spectacular views and opportunities for birdwatching and photography. The island's volcanic origins have also created a number of caves and grottos along the coast, adding to the area's natural allure.

Top Nature Reserves and Protected Areas in Lipari

1. Montagna della Guardia

Montagna della Guardia, the highest point on Lipari, is a designated nature reserve that offers breathtaking views and a variety of hiking trails.

- **Location:** Southern part of Lipari, near the village of Quattropani.
- **What to Expect:** The reserve encompasses the volcanic peak of Montagna della Guardia, which rises to an elevation of 602 meters. The area is crisscrossed with trails that lead through dense Mediterranean vegetation, offering

panoramic views of the surrounding islands and the Tyrrhenian Sea.
- **Flora and Fauna:** The reserve is home to a variety of plant species, including endemic shrubs and wildflowers. Birdwatchers can spot a range of species, including kestrels, falcons, and migratory birds during the spring and autumn months.
- **Highlights:** The summit of Montagna della Guardia offers one of the best viewpoints on the island, with unobstructed views of Lipari and the other Aeolian Islands. The area is also a great spot for stargazing, thanks to its remote location and minimal light pollution.

2. Valle Muria

Valle Muria is a protected area that combines the beauty of Lipari's coastal landscape with the tranquility of its natural surroundings.

- **Location:** Southwestern coast of Lipari.
- **What to Expect:** Valle Muria is known for its stunning beach, surrounded by steep cliffs and accessible via a scenic path. The area is relatively secluded, offering a peaceful retreat for those looking to escape the more crowded parts of the island.
- **Flora and Fauna:** The cliffs and surrounding areas are home to a variety of plant species, including wild herbs and Mediterranean shrubs. The beach itself is a great spot for observing marine life, with clear waters that are perfect for snorkeling.
- **Highlights:** The dramatic cliffs and crystal-clear waters of Valle Muria make it one of the most picturesque spots on

the island. The area is also an excellent place for a quiet hike, with paths leading through the rugged landscape to viewpoints overlooking the sea.

3. Punta del Perciato

Punta del Perciato is a protected coastal area known for its unique volcanic formations and rich marine life.

- **Location:** Southeastern coast of Lipari.
- **What to Expect:** The area is famous for its natural arch, a striking rock formation created by volcanic activity. The coastline here is rugged and rocky, with clear waters that are ideal for swimming and snorkeling.
- **Flora and Fauna:** The rocky terrain supports a range of plant species adapted to the harsh coastal environment. In the waters surrounding Punta del Perciato, you'll find a variety of fish, crustaceans, and other marine creatures, making it a popular spot for snorkeling and diving.
- **Highlights:** The natural arch at Punta del Perciato is one of Lipari's most iconic landmarks. The area is also a great place for photography, with the dramatic volcanic landscape providing a stunning backdrop.

4. Pumice Quarries

The Pumice Quarries of Lipari, while not a traditional nature reserve, are a unique geological site that offers insight into the island's volcanic history.

- **Location:** Northern coast of Lipari, near Acquacalda.
- **What to Expect:** The quarries are characterized by their white pumice cliffs, which have been mined for centuries.

The area is a fascinating blend of natural beauty and industrial history, with the white cliffs contrasting sharply with the blue of the sea.
- **Flora and Fauna:** The harsh, rocky environment around the quarries supports a limited range of plant life, but the area is rich in geological features. The surrounding waters are home to a variety of marine species, making it a popular spot for snorkeling.
- **Highlights:** The Pumice Quarries offer a unique landscape that is unlike anything else on the island. The white pumice cliffs are particularly striking at sunset when the light enhances their brilliant whiteness.

Activities in Lipari's Nature Reserves and Protected Areas

1. **Hiking and Walking:**
    - **Trail Networks:** Lipari's nature reserves offer a variety of hiking trails, ranging from easy walks to more challenging hikes. These trails provide access to some of the island's most beautiful natural areas, with opportunities to see rare plants, birds, and geological formations.
    - **Guided Walks:** For those interested in learning more about the island's natural environment, guided walks are available. These tours are led by knowledgeable guides who can provide insight into the flora, fauna, and geological history of the area.
2. **Birdwatching:**
    - **Bird Species:** Lipari is a great destination for birdwatching, with a variety of species that can be spotted throughout the year. The island's nature

reserves provide excellent opportunities to see raptors, seabirds, and migratory species.
  - **Best Spots:** The cliffs of Valle Muria and the summit of Montagna della Guardia are particularly good for birdwatching, offering the chance to see both resident and migratory birds.
3. **Marine Activities:**
   - **Snorkeling and Diving:** Lipari's protected coastal areas offer some of the best snorkeling and diving opportunities in the Aeolian Islands. The clear waters and rich marine life make for an unforgettable underwater experience.
   - **Boat Tours:** Exploring Lipari's coastline by boat is a great way to see the island's natural beauty from a different perspective. Boat tours often include stops at key nature reserves and marine protected areas, allowing visitors to swim, snorkel, or simply enjoy the scenery.

Conservation Efforts and Environmental Responsibility

Lipari's nature reserves and protected areas are crucial for conserving the island's natural heritage. Visitors are encouraged to respect these areas by following guidelines and practicing sustainable tourism.

- **Respect for Nature:** Stick to designated trails, avoid disturbing wildlife, and do not pick plants or collect stones. These practices help preserve the delicate ecosystems that make Lipari special.
- **Waste Management:** Always carry out what you carry in. Littering can have a significant impact on the environment, particularly in fragile ecosystems.

- **Support Local Conservation:** Consider supporting local conservation efforts by participating in eco-friendly tours, making donations to conservation organizations, or simply spreading awareness about the importance of protecting Lipari's natural environment.

LIPARI'S CULINARY SCENE

Lipari offers a culinary experience that is as rich and diverse as its history and landscapes. The island's cuisine is deeply rooted in tradition, blending Mediterranean flavors with local ingredients, and influenced by the various cultures that have passed through the region over the centuries. From fresh seafood to fragrant herbs and sun-ripened produce, every meal in Lipari is a celebration of the island's natural bounty.

The Essence of Lipari's Cuisine

The food of Lipari is characterized by simplicity and freshness. The island's volcanic soil, coupled with its mild climate, produces some of the best fruits, vegetables, and herbs in the Mediterranean. These ingredients form the backbone of Lipari's culinary offerings

1. Fresh Seafood

- **A Maritime Tradition:** Given Lipari's location in the heart of the Tyrrhenian Sea, it's no surprise that seafood plays a central role in the island's cuisine. Fresh catches such as swordfish, tuna, and anchovies are staples, often grilled or served in light, flavorful sauces.
- **Signature Dishes:** Dishes like "pasta con le sarde" (pasta with sardines) and "insalata di polpo" (octopus salad) showcase the island's seafood heritage. Another popular dish is "spaghetti alla Liparota," featuring tomatoes, capers, olives, and fresh fish.

2. Local Produce

- **Sun-Kissed Ingredients:** Lipari's fertile soil yields an abundance of fresh produce, including tomatoes, eggplants, peppers, and zucchini. These ingredients are often used in simple yet delicious preparations, such as "caponata," a sweet and sour eggplant dish, or grilled vegetables drizzled with olive oil.
- **Herbs and Seasonings:** Aromatic herbs like oregano, basil, and rosemary are frequently used to enhance the flavors of dishes. The use of capers, which grow wild on the island, is another hallmark of Lipari's cuisine.

3. Traditional Recipes

- **Cultural Fusion:** Lipari's cuisine reflects the island's diverse cultural influences, from ancient Greek and Roman to Arabic and Spanish. This fusion is evident in dishes like "cuscus alla Trapanese," a couscous dish with a distinctly Sicilian twist, or "pani cunzatu," a traditional bread topped with olive oil, tomatoes, and anchovies.
- **Family Recipes:** Many of Lipari's best dishes are based on recipes passed down through generations. These time-honored recipes are often simple but rely on the quality of the ingredients to shine.

Dining Experiences on Lipari

Eating in Lipari is not just about the food; it's also about the setting and the experience. Whether you're dining at a beachside restaurant with your toes in the sand or enjoying a meal in a rustic trattoria in the heart of the town, the atmosphere adds to the enjoyment of the meal.

1. **Seaside Dining**

   - **Ocean Views:** Many of Lipari's restaurants offer stunning views of the sea, providing the perfect backdrop for a leisurely meal. The sound of the waves and the scent of the sea breeze enhance the dining experience, making every bite taste even better.
   - **Fresh Off the Boat:** Some restaurants offer the day's catch, allowing you to enjoy the freshest seafood possible. It's not uncommon for the menu to change daily, depending on what the fishermen have brought in.

2. **Trattorias and Family-Owned Restaurants**

   - **Authentic Flavors:** For a more traditional experience, head to one of Lipari's family-owned trattorias. These establishments often serve homemade dishes that have been perfected over generations. The portions are generous, and the atmosphere is warm and welcoming.
   - **Local Hospitality:** In these intimate settings, you'll often be treated like family. The owners may take the time to explain the origins of the dishes, share stories about the island, and offer recommendations for the best local wines to accompany your meal.

3. **Street Food and Markets**

   - **Quick Bites:** If you're looking for a more casual dining experience, Lipari's street food scene offers plenty of options. From "arancini" (stuffed rice balls) to "panelle" (chickpea fritters), these portable treats are perfect for enjoying on the go.

- **Fresh and Local:** Don't miss the chance to visit one of the island's markets, where you can sample fresh produce, cheeses, and cured meats. The market is also a great place to pick up local specialties to take home as souvenirs.

Wines and Beverages

Lipari's culinary scene would not be complete without its wines and beverages, which are as much a part of the island's heritage as its food. The island's volcanic soil and favorable climate produce wines with distinct flavors, often enjoyed alongside the local cuisine.

1. Malvasia delle Lipari

- **A Sweet Tradition:** Malvasia is Lipari's signature wine, a sweet dessert wine made from sun-dried grapes. This wine has been produced on the island for centuries and is often enjoyed as an after-dinner treat or paired with desserts.
- **Tasting Experiences:** Many local wineries offer tastings, allowing you to sample different varieties of Malvasia along with other wines produced on the island. These tastings are often accompanied by small plates of local delicacies, enhancing the experience.

2. Local Wines

- **Volcanic Influence:** The volcanic soil of Lipari contributes to the unique characteristics of the island's wines. In addition to Malvasia, Lipari produces a range of red and white wines that pair beautifully with the local cuisine.
- **Wine Tours:** Consider taking a wine tour to explore the vineyards and learn more about the winemaking process.

These tours often include visits to small, family-owned wineries where you can meet the winemakers and hear their stories.

3. Aperitivo Culture

- **Evening Ritual:** The tradition of aperitivo is alive and well in Lipari. As the sun sets, locals and visitors alike gather in cafes and bars to enjoy a pre-dinner drink and small bites. Popular choices include "Aperol Spritz," local wines, or a refreshing glass of "granita," a semi-frozen dessert made from sugar, water, and various flavorings.
- **Social Experience:** Aperitivo is as much about socializing as it is about the drinks and food. It's a time to relax, chat with friends, and soak in the island's vibrant atmosphere.

Traditional Eolian Cuisine

The cuisine of the Aeolian Islands, particularly Lipari, is a delightful fusion of Mediterranean flavors, enriched by centuries of history and cultural influences. Traditional Eolian cuisine is characterized by its simplicity, reliance on fresh, local ingredients, and the unique blend of flavors that reflect the island's maritime and volcanic heritage. Whether you're dining in a rustic trattoria or sampling street food by the sea, the flavors of Lipari offer a culinary journey that is both authentic and unforgettable.

Key Ingredients and Flavors

Eolian cuisine is a celebration of the island's natural bounty, with dishes that highlight the best of what the land and sea have to offer. The ingredients used are often grown locally or sourced from the surrounding waters, ensuring freshness and flavor.

1. **Seafood**

    - **Foundation of the Cuisine:** Given Lipari's location in the heart of the Mediterranean, seafood is the cornerstone of traditional Eolian dishes. Freshly caught fish, squid, octopus, and shellfish are commonly used, often prepared simply to let the natural flavors shine.
    - **Signature Seafood Dishes:** Popular dishes include "pesce spada alla griglia" (grilled swordfish), "calamari ripieni" (stuffed squid), and "tonno al sesamo" (sesame-crusted tuna). Another local favorite is "zuppa di pesce," a hearty fish stew that showcases a variety of seafood in a rich tomato broth.

2. **Vegetables and Herbs**

    - **Sun-Ripened Produce:** The volcanic soil and sunny climate of the Aeolian Islands produce an abundance of flavorful vegetables. Tomatoes, eggplants, zucchini, and peppers are staples, often grilled, roasted, or used in stews and salads.
    - **Herbaceous Touch:** Fresh herbs play a significant role in Eolian cuisine. Oregano, basil, mint, and rosemary are frequently used to season dishes, adding aromatic depth and complexity.

3. **Capers**

    - **A Local Specialty:** Capers are one of Lipari's most famous exports, growing wild across the island. These small, tangy buds are harvested and preserved in salt or vinegar, adding a distinctive flavor to many Eolian dishes.

- **Caper-Based Dishes:** "Insalata eoliana" is a classic dish that features capers prominently, along with tomatoes, olives, and onions. Capers are also used to garnish seafood dishes, pasta, and salads, providing a burst of flavor that is quintessentially Eolian.

4. Olives and Olive Oil

- **Golden Liquid:** Olive oil is the primary cooking fat in Eolian cuisine, used in everything from frying to drizzling over finished dishes. The island's olives are also enjoyed as appetizers, either cured or stuffed.
- **Olio Novello:** During the olive harvest in late autumn, the first pressing of the season, known as "olio novello," is a highly anticipated event. This fresh, vibrant olive oil is celebrated for its intense flavor and is often enjoyed simply with bread.

5. Bread and Pasta

- **Rustic Breads:** Bread is a staple of the Eolian diet, with local varieties often baked in wood-fired ovens. "Pane cunzatu," a traditional Eolian bread topped with tomatoes, capers, anchovies, and olive oil, is a must-try.
- **Homemade Pasta:** Eolian cuisine features a variety of pasta dishes, often served with simple sauces that highlight the flavors of the sea. "Pasta alla Liparota," made with capers, olives, tomatoes, and anchovies, is a local specialty.

Traditional Eolian Dishes

1. Caponata Eoliana:

- **A Sweet and Sour Delight:** This classic dish is a flavorful mix of eggplant, tomatoes, capers, olives, and onions, cooked in a sweet and sour sauce. The Eolian version of caponata is distinguished by the addition of capers and sometimes raisins or pine nuts, giving it a unique twist.
- **Versatile Serving:** Caponata is typically served as an appetizer or side dish, but it can also be enjoyed as a light meal with crusty bread.

2. Coniglio alla Pignata:

- **Rabbit Stew:** "Coniglio alla pignata" is a traditional Eolian dish featuring rabbit slow-cooked in a clay pot with tomatoes, olives, capers, and aromatic herbs. The result is a tender, flavorful stew that is both hearty and satisfying.
- **Rustic Roots:** This dish is a testament to the island's agricultural past, where rabbits were a common source of protein. The slow cooking method allows the flavors to meld together beautifully, creating a dish that is rich in taste and history.

3. Alici Arriganate:

- **Marinated Anchovies:** This dish showcases the simplicity and flavor of fresh anchovies, marinated in lemon juice, olive oil, garlic, and herbs. "Alici arriganate" is a popular antipasto in Lipari, offering a zesty, refreshing start to a meal.

- **Traditional Preparation:** The anchovies are typically filleted and layered in a dish with the marinade, then left to soak up the flavors before being served with crusty bread.

4. Fritto Misto:

- **Mixed Fried Seafood:** "Fritto misto" is a delightful medley of lightly battered and fried seafood, including shrimp, squid, and small fish. This dish is often served with a wedge of lemon and is a favorite among locals and visitors alike.
- **Crispy and Light:** The key to a perfect fritto misto is the freshness of the seafood and the lightness of the batter, which ensures a crispy, golden finish.

5. Cassata Eoliana:

- **A Sweet Treat:** For dessert, the Eolian version of cassata, a traditional Sicilian cake, is a must-try. "Cassata Eoliana" is a rich, layered cake made with ricotta cheese, sponge cake, marzipan, and candied fruit.
- **Colorful and Festive:** This dessert is not only delicious but also visually stunning, often decorated with bright, colorful fruits and marzipan, making it a centerpiece at celebrations.

Eolian Beverages

No discussion of Eolian cuisine would be complete without mentioning the island's beverages, particularly its wines and liqueurs.

1. Malvasia delle Lipari:

- **Sweet Nectar:** "Malvasia delle Lipari" is the island's signature wine, a sweet dessert wine made from sun-dried grapes. It has a rich, honeyed flavor with notes of apricot, raisins, and citrus, making it a perfect accompaniment to desserts or enjoyed on its own.
- **Heritage and Craftsmanship:** This wine has been produced in Lipari for centuries, with traditional methods passed down through generations. Many local wineries offer tastings, providing an opportunity to learn about the winemaking process and the history of this beloved wine.

2. Amaro Eoliano:

- **Herbal Liqueur:** "Amaro Eoliano" is a traditional herbal liqueur made with a blend of local herbs, roots, and spices. It is typically enjoyed as a digestif after a meal, offering a bittersweet flavor that is both refreshing and complex.
- **A Taste of the Islands:** This liqueur reflects the island's rich natural environment, with ingredients that are often foraged from the surrounding landscape.

Top Restaurants and Eateries in Lipari

Lipari is a haven for food lovers. The island's rich culinary traditions, stunning views, and warm hospitality make dining here a memorable experience. From fine dining establishments to cozy trattorias, Lipari offers a diverse range of dining options that cater to all tastes and budgets. Here's a guide to some of the top restaurants and eateries on the island.

Fine Dining and Upscale Restaurants

For those looking to indulge in a gourmet meal, Lipari boasts several fine dining establishments where the island's culinary traditions are elevated with modern techniques and presentation. These restaurants offer not only exceptional food but also impeccable service and breathtaking views.

1. Ristorante Filippino:

- **A Historical Gem:** Established in 1910, Ristorante Filippino is one of the oldest and most renowned restaurants on the island. It has a long-standing reputation for serving exquisite Eolian cuisine, with a focus on fresh seafood and traditional dishes prepared with a modern twist.
- **Signature Dishes:** The menu features a variety of delicacies, including "linguine al pesto eoliano" (linguine with Aeolian pesto) and "pesce spada alla griglia" (grilled swordfish). The restaurant also offers an extensive wine list, featuring local and regional wines.
- **Ambiance:** The elegant dining room and outdoor terrace provide a perfect setting for a special evening, offering views of the marina and the surrounding hills.

2. Ristorante La Conchiglia:

- **Seaside Elegance:** Located in the Canneto area, Ristorante La Conchiglia is known for its beautiful beachfront location and sophisticated atmosphere. The restaurant specializes in seafood, with a menu that highlights the freshest catches of the day.

- **Must-Try Dishes:** Diners can enjoy dishes such as "spaghetti alle vongole" (spaghetti with clams) and "gamberoni alla griglia" (grilled prawns). The restaurant's signature dish, "risotto ai frutti di mare" (seafood risotto), is a particular favorite.
- **Atmosphere:** The open-air terrace, with its panoramic views of the sea, is the perfect spot for a romantic dinner or a leisurely lunch.

3. **Ristorante E Pulera:**

- **A Garden Oasis:** Set in a charming garden filled with lemon trees, Ristorante E Pulera offers a serene and intimate dining experience. The restaurant prides itself on its farm-to-table approach, using locally sourced ingredients to create dishes that are both traditional and innovative.
- **Culinary Highlights:** The menu includes specialties such as "maccheroni al sugo di cernia" (pasta with grouper sauce) and "involtini di pesce spada" (swordfish rolls). The desserts, particularly the "cassata eoliana," are not to be missed.
- **Setting:** The lush garden setting, combined with the attentive service, makes dining at Ristorante E Pulera a truly memorable experience.

Cozy Trattorias and Local Favorites

For a more casual dining experience, Lipari offers a wealth of trattorias and family-run restaurants where you can enjoy hearty, home-cooked meals in a relaxed atmosphere. These eateries are the heart of Lipari's culinary scene, offering authentic dishes that have been passed down through generations.

1. Trattoria del Vicolo:

- **Authentic Flavors:** Tucked away in a charming alley in the heart of Lipari town, Trattoria del Vicolo is a local favorite known for its warm hospitality and traditional Eolian cuisine. The menu features a range of dishes made with fresh, local ingredients, prepared with love and care.
- **Popular Choices:** Highlights include "pasta alla norma" (pasta with eggplant, tomatoes, and ricotta salata) and "calamari ripieni" (stuffed calamari). The restaurant also offers a selection of house-made desserts, such as "tiramisu al limone."
- **Ambiance:** The intimate setting, with its rustic decor and outdoor seating, makes it a perfect spot for a cozy meal with friends or family.

2. Pizzeria Il Corallo:

- **Casual and Fun:** For those craving a delicious pizza, Pizzeria Il Corallo is the place to go. This lively eatery serves up a variety of wood-fired pizzas, with toppings ranging from classic Margherita to more adventurous combinations featuring local ingredients.
- **Pizza Perfection:** In addition to pizza, the menu includes pasta dishes, salads, and antipasti. The "pizza alla Eoliana," topped with tomatoes, capers, olives, and anchovies, is a must-try.
- **Atmosphere:** The casual, laid-back vibe and friendly service make Pizzeria Il Corallo a great choice for a relaxed evening out.

3. **Trattoria A' Sfiziusa:**

- **Home-Style Cooking:** Trattoria A' Sfiziusa is a hidden gem, offering simple, yet flavorful dishes that showcase the best of Eolian home cooking. The restaurant is known for its generous portions and reasonable prices, making it a popular choice among locals and visitors alike.
- **Recommended Dishes:** The menu changes daily, depending on what's fresh and in season, but staples like "spaghetti alle sarde" (spaghetti with sardines) and "insalata di polpo" (octopus salad) are always crowd-pleasers.
- **Family Atmosphere:** The warm, welcoming atmosphere, combined with the delicious food, makes Trattoria A' Sfiziusa feel like a home away from home.

Street Food and Casual Eateries

For a quick bite or a more informal dining experience, Lipari has plenty of options that allow you to enjoy the island's flavors on the go. From street food vendors to casual cafes, these spots are perfect for a snack or a light meal.

1. Pasticceria Subba:

- **Sweet Treats:** No visit to Lipari would be complete without sampling some of the island's famous pastries, and Pasticceria Subba is the place to do it. This beloved bakery offers a wide range of sweet delights, from "cannoli" and "cassata" to "granita" and "brioche."
- **Signature Sweets:** The "granita al limone" (lemon granita) is a refreshing treat on a hot day, while the "cannoli" are

filled with rich, creamy ricotta and dusted with powdered sugar.
- **Grab and Go:** Whether you're stopping in for a quick espresso and pastry or picking up treats to enjoy later, Pasticceria Subba is a must-visit for anyone with a sweet tooth.

2. Il Galeone:

- **Quick and Delicious:** Located near the port, Il Galeone is a casual eatery that offers a variety of sandwiches, salads, and light meals, perfect for a quick bite before or after exploring the island. The menu focuses on fresh, local ingredients, with an emphasis on seafood.
- **Popular Items:** The "panino con pesce spada" (swordfish sandwich) is a favorite, as is the "insalata di mare" (seafood salad). The eatery also offers a selection of refreshing drinks and gelato.
- **Convenient Location:** With its prime location and speedy service, Il Galeone is ideal for travelers on the go who still want to enjoy a taste of Lipari.

3. Bar La Precchia:

- **Classic Italian Bar:** For a true Italian experience, stop by Bar La Precchia, where you can enjoy an espresso or an aperitivo while soaking in the local atmosphere. The bar also serves light snacks, such as panini and pastries, making it a great spot for a casual breakfast or afternoon break.

- **Sip and Savor:** In the evening, the bar is a popular spot for aperitivo, where you can enjoy a spritz or a glass of local wine along with a selection of small bites.
- **Local Hangout:** The laid-back vibe and friendly service make Bar La Precchia a favorite among both locals and tourists.

Food Markets and Street Food in Lipari

Lipari is a paradise for food lovers seeking authentic local flavors and fresh produce. The island's markets and street food offer a glimpse into the daily life of its inhabitants, providing visitors with the opportunity to sample traditional dishes, buy fresh ingredients, and immerse themselves in the vibrant culinary culture of Lipari. Here's a comprehensive guide to exploring the food markets and street food scene on the island.

Exploring Lipari's Food Markets

Lipari's food markets are the heart of the island's culinary life, bustling with activity and filled with the colors, aromas, and flavors of the Mediterranean. These markets are the perfect place to discover fresh produce, local specialties, and seasonal ingredients, all of which play a crucial role in Eolian cuisine.

1. Mercato di Lipari:

- **The Central Market:** Located in Lipari town, the Mercato di Lipari is the island's main food market, where locals and visitors alike come to shop for fresh fruits, vegetables, seafood, meats, and other local products. The market is a lively and colorful place, with vendors offering a wide variety of goods, from freshly caught fish to sun-ripened tomatoes.
- **What to Buy:** At the market, you'll find an array of local produce, such as capers, olives, and lemons, as well as fresh herbs like oregano and basil. The seafood stalls are particularly popular, offering everything from swordfish to octopus, all caught in the surrounding waters. Don't miss the opportunity to buy some local cheeses, such as ricotta

salata or pecorino, which pair perfectly with the island's wine.
- **Market Experience:** The Mercato di Lipari is not just a place to shop but also a place to experience the island's culture. Engage with the friendly vendors, sample some of the produce, and soak in the lively atmosphere. The market is typically open in the mornings, so it's a great way to start your day on the island.

2. Farmer's Market:

- **A Taste of the Countryside:** Held weekly, the Farmer's Market in Lipari is a smaller, more intimate market that focuses on locally grown produce and artisanal products. This market is a great place to buy organic fruits and vegetables, homemade jams, olive oil, and other delicacies directly from the producers.
- **Seasonal Offerings:** Depending on the time of year, you'll find different seasonal products at the Farmer's Market. In the summer, expect to see an abundance of tomatoes, zucchini, and eggplants, while in the fall, you might find fresh figs, grapes, and chestnuts. The market also features stalls selling freshly baked bread, pastries, and traditional Eolian sweets.
- **Local Interactions:** The Farmer's Market is a wonderful opportunity to meet local farmers and artisans, learn about their products, and gain insights into the island's agricultural traditions. It's a more relaxed and personal experience compared to the larger central market.

Street Food in Lipari

Street food is an integral part of Lipari's culinary scene, offering quick, affordable, and delicious options for those on the go. Whether you're exploring the island's charming streets or relaxing by the beach, you'll find plenty of opportunities to sample the island's street food.

1. Pane Cunzato:

- **The Iconic Sandwich:** Pane cunzato is one of Lipari's most beloved street foods, a traditional sandwich that showcases the island's simple yet flavorful ingredients. It's made with rustic bread, usually topped with tomatoes, olives, capers, anchovies, and a drizzle of olive oil, then baked or grilled until the bread is crispy and the toppings are warm.
- **Where to Find It:** You'll find pane cunzato at bakeries, food stalls, and small eateries throughout Lipari. It's the perfect snack to take with you while exploring the island or enjoying a day at the beach.
- **A Taste of Tradition:** Pane cunzato is a quintessential example of Eolian cuisine, emphasizing the use of fresh, local ingredients. It's a must-try for anyone visiting the island.

2. Arancini:

- **Sicilian Influence:** Arancini, the famous Sicilian rice balls, are also popular in Lipari. These golden, fried balls of rice are typically stuffed with a variety of fillings, such as ragu (meat sauce), mozzarella, or peas. They are crispy on the outside and soft and savory on the inside.

- **Street Food Staple:** Arancini are a common sight at street food stalls and cafes on the island, and they make for a satisfying and portable meal. Whether you enjoy them as a quick snack or a light lunch, arancini are sure to delight your taste buds.
- **Variations:** While the classic ragu-filled arancini is the most popular, you may also find variations with fillings like ham and cheese, or even sweet versions filled with chocolate or pistachio cream.

3. **Granita:**

- **Refreshing Treat:** Granita is a traditional Sicilian frozen dessert that is also widely enjoyed in Lipari. Made from sugar, water, and fruit flavors, granita is similar to a sorbet but has a coarser, more crystalline texture. It's the perfect way to cool down on a hot day.
- **Popular Flavors:** The most common flavors of granita in Lipari are lemon, almond, and mulberry, but you may also find other fruit flavors depending on the season. Granita is often served with a brioche, a soft, sweet bread roll, making it a popular breakfast or snack.
- **Where to Find It:** You can find granita at cafes, bars, and street vendors throughout the island. It's a refreshing and flavorful treat that you can enjoy while taking in the sights of Lipari.

4. **Panelle and Crocchè:**

- **Sicilian Snacks:** Panelle and crocchè are two more examples of Sicilian street food that have found their way to Lipari. Panelle are thin, fried chickpea flour fritters,

while crocchè are potato croquettes, often filled with cheese or herbs. Both are delicious, savory snacks that are perfect for a quick bite.
- **Street Vendor Favorites:** These snacks are commonly sold by street vendors or in small eateries, often served in a sandwich or on their own. They are particularly popular as a mid-morning or afternoon snack.
- **Crispy and Flavorful:** The combination of crispy, golden exterior and soft, flavorful interior makes panelle and crocchè irresistible. Pair them with a cold drink for the ultimate street food experience.

Wine Tasting and Local Vineyards in Lipari

Lipari is not just a destination for stunning landscapes and rich history—it's also a treasure trove for wine enthusiasts. The island, with its volcanic soil, Mediterranean climate, and centuries-old winemaking traditions, produces some of Italy's most unique and flavorful wines. Exploring the vineyards and engaging in wine tasting experiences is a must for visitors looking to immerse themselves in the local culture. Here's a comprehensive guide to wine tasting and the local vineyards of Lipari.

The Winemaking Tradition in Lipari

The Aeolian Islands, including Lipari, have a winemaking history that dates back to ancient times. The volcanic soil, rich in minerals, combined with the island's sunny climate and cooling sea breezes, creates ideal conditions for growing grapes. These unique conditions impart distinctive flavors and characteristics to the wines, making Aeolian wines truly special.

1. Historical Roots:

- **Ancient Origins:** The tradition of winemaking in Lipari can be traced back to the ancient Greeks, who colonized the islands and introduced viticulture. Over the centuries, winemaking has evolved, but the connection to the land and the use of traditional methods remain central to the production of wine in Lipari.
- **Volcanic Influence:** The volcanic soil of Lipari, rich in minerals like potassium and phosphorus, gives the grapes a unique flavor profile. This terroir, combined with the island's microclimate, results in wines that are often described as having a distinct minerality and freshness.

2. **Traditional Grape Varieties:**

- **Malvasia delle Lipari:** The most famous grape variety grown on Lipari is Malvasia delle Lipari, a white grape known for producing aromatic, sweet wines. This grape is the cornerstone of the island's winemaking tradition and is used to produce both dry and sweet wines, including the renowned Malvasia delle Lipari Passito, a dessert wine made from partially dried grapes.
- **Corinto Nero and Nocera:** In addition to Malvasia, other traditional grape varieties such as Corinto Nero and Nocera are also cultivated on the island. These red grapes contribute to the production of robust, full-bodied wines with deep color and complex flavors.

1. **Tenuta di Castellaro:**

- **A Scenic Vineyard:** One of the most renowned wineries on Lipari, Tenuta di Castellaro is located on the slopes of Mount Pelato, offering breathtaking views of the surrounding islands and the Tyrrhenian Sea. This family-owned estate is dedicated to producing organic wines that reflect the unique terroir of Lipari.

- **Wine Tasting and Tours:** Visitors to Tenuta di Castellaro can take guided tours of the vineyard and the winery, where they'll learn about the organic farming practices and traditional winemaking techniques used to produce the estate's wines. The tour typically concludes with a wine tasting session, where you can sample a variety of wines, including the estate's signature Malvasia delle Lipari and Nero Ossidiana, a red wine blend of Corinto Nero and Nocera.
- **A Memorable Experience:** The tasting sessions are often held on the estate's panoramic terrace, allowing you to enjoy the wines while taking in the stunning views of the island's landscape. The winery also offers food pairings, such as local cheeses, cured meats, and olives, to complement the wines.

2. **Cantina Caravaglio:**

- **Organic Winemaking:** Cantina Caravaglio is another prominent winery in Lipari, known for its commitment to organic viticulture and sustainable farming practices. The Caravaglio family has been producing wine on the island for generations, and their dedication to quality and tradition is evident in every bottle.
- **Tasting Room Experience:** At Cantina Caravaglio, visitors can enjoy a personalized wine tasting experience in the estate's tasting room or outdoor patio. The winery produces a range of wines, including the elegant Malvasia

delle Lipari, as well as unique blends that highlight the diversity of the island's grape varieties.
- **Vineyard Tours:** In addition to tastings, the winery offers guided tours of the vineyards, where you can learn about the organic farming practices and the influence of the volcanic soil on the grapes. The tour provides a deeper understanding of the connection between the land and the wine, making the tasting experience even more enriching.

3. Az. Agricola Punta Aria:

- **Boutique Winery:** Az. Agricola Punta Aria is a small, family-run winery located in a picturesque setting on Lipari. Despite its size, the winery is known for producing high-quality wines that capture the essence of the island's terroir.
- **Intimate Tastings:** The winery offers intimate wine tastings in a cozy setting, where you can sample their limited-production wines, including a delicate Malvasia delle Lipari and a robust red made from Corinto Nero grapes. The tastings are often accompanied by local snacks, such as freshly baked bread, olive oil, and capers.
- **Authentic Experience:** A visit to Az. Agricola Punta Aria provides an authentic glimpse into the small-scale, artisanal approach to winemaking that is still practiced on Lipari. The owners are often on hand to share stories about the vineyard and the winemaking process, making it a personalized and memorable experience.

Local Wine Festivals and Events

In addition to vineyard tours and tastings, Lipari also hosts several wine-related events throughout the year, providing visitors with even more opportunities to explore the island's wines.

1. Malvasia Wine Festival:

- **Celebrating Malvasia:** The Malvasia Wine Festival is an annual event that takes place on Lipari and the other Aeolian Islands, celebrating the island's most famous wine. The festival features wine tastings, workshops, and cultural events that highlight the history and production of Malvasia delle Lipari.
- **Cultural Experience:** The festival is a wonderful opportunity to immerse yourself in the local culture, meet winemakers, and taste a variety of Malvasia wines, including rare and limited-edition bottles. The event also includes traditional music, dance, and food, making it a lively and festive occasion.

2. Cantine Aperte:

- **Open Cellars:** Cantine Aperte, or Open Cellars, is a nationwide event in Italy where wineries open their doors to the public for tours and tastings. On Lipari, several wineries participate in this event, offering visitors a chance to explore the island's vineyards, learn about the winemaking process, and sample a wide range of wines.
- **Interactive Experience:** Cantine Aperte is an interactive experience that often includes guided walks through the vineyards, demonstrations of traditional winemaking techniques, and opportunities to purchase wines directly from the producers.

CULTURE AND FESTIVALS IN LIPARI

Lipari is a place where centuries-old traditions and vibrant cultural expressions thrive. The island's rich history, shaped by various civilizations, is reflected in its unique cultural practices and lively festivals that draw both locals and visitors into a shared celebration of heritage. Exploring Lipari's culture and festivals offers a deeper understanding of the island's identity and provides unforgettable experiences for those fortunate enough to partake.

Cultural Heritage of Lipari

Lipari's cultural fabric is woven from the threads of its diverse history, influenced by the Greeks, Romans, Byzantines, Arabs, Normans, and other peoples who have left their mark on the island. This mosaic of influences is evident in the island's architecture, religious practices, art, music, and daily life.

1. A Blend of Influences:

- **Historical Layers:** The architecture of Lipari, with its ancient ruins, medieval castles, and baroque churches, tells the story of the island's complex history. Each era has contributed to the island's cultural landscape, creating a unique blend of styles and traditions that are still evident today.
- **Religious Significance:** Religion plays a central role in the cultural life of Lipari, with Catholicism being the predominant faith. The island is dotted with beautiful churches, each with its own historical and spiritual significance. Religious festivals and processions, which often involve the entire community, are a key aspect of Lipari's cultural identity.

2. Art and Craftsmanship:

- **Artistic Traditions:** Lipari has a long tradition of craftsmanship, particularly in ceramics and pottery, which dates back to ancient times. The island's artisans produce a wide range of handmade goods, from intricate ceramics to woven textiles, which reflect the island's cultural heritage.
- **Contemporary Art:** In addition to traditional crafts, Lipari has a thriving contemporary art scene. Local artists and galleries showcase works that often draw inspiration from the island's natural beauty and historical legacy, blending modern techniques with traditional themes.

Festivals in Lipari

Festivals are a vibrant expression of Lipari's culture, offering a glimpse into the island's traditions, religious devotion, and communal spirit. These events, which range from solemn religious observances to lively cultural celebrations, are an integral part of life on the island.

1. Feast of San Bartolomeo:

- **Patron Saint Celebration:** The Feast of San Bartolomeo, held every year on August 24th, is the most important religious festival on Lipari. San Bartolomeo, or Saint Bartholomew, is the island's patron saint, and his feast day is marked by a series of religious ceremonies, processions, and festive activities.
- **Religious Procession:** The highlight of the festival is the solemn procession through the streets of Lipari, where a statue of San Bartolomeo is carried by the faithful,

accompanied by music and prayers. The procession ends at the Cathedral of San Bartolomeo, where a special mass is held.
- **Fireworks and Festivities:** The religious observances are complemented by a lively program of events, including music, dancing, and a spectacular fireworks display over the harbor. The festival is a time of joy and celebration, bringing together the entire community in a shared expression of faith and tradition.

2. **Aeolian Film Festival:**

- **Celebrating Cinema:** The Aeolian Film Festival, held annually on Lipari, is a cultural event that showcases films from around the world, with a special focus on works that explore themes related to the sea, islands, and the environment. The festival attracts filmmakers, critics, and cinema enthusiasts, making it a significant event on the island's cultural calendar.
- **Screenings and Events:** The festival features outdoor screenings in picturesque locations, workshops, panel discussions, and Q&A sessions with filmmakers. It's an opportunity for visitors to engage with the world of cinema while enjoying the stunning backdrop of Lipari's landscapes.
- **Cultural Exchange:** The Aeolian Film Festival also serves as a platform for cultural exchange, fostering connections between the local community and international artists. It highlights the importance of preserving the natural and cultural heritage of the Aeolian Islands through the medium of film.

3. **Carnival of Lipari:**

   - **Colorful Revelry:** Carnival is a time of exuberant celebration on Lipari, with the island coming alive with colorful costumes, parades, music, and dancing. Held in the weeks leading up to Lent, the Carnival of Lipari is a joyful event that reflects the island's festive spirit and love of tradition.
   - **Parades and Masks:** The highlight of the carnival is the grand parade, where participants don elaborate masks and costumes, often inspired by historical or mythological themes. The parade winds through the streets of Lipari, accompanied by lively music and dancing, creating a festive atmosphere that is infectious.
   - **Community Involvement:** Carnival is a community-wide event, with people of all ages taking part in the celebrations. It's a time for creativity, laughter, and coming together, making it one of the most anticipated events of the year.

4. **Festival of the Sea:**

   - **Honoring Maritime Heritage:** The Festival of the Sea is a celebration of Lipari's deep connection to the sea, which has shaped the island's culture and way of life for centuries. Held in the summer, this festival features a variety of activities that highlight the island's maritime traditions, including boat races, fishing competitions, and seafood feasts.
   - **Cultural Exhibitions:** The festival also includes cultural exhibitions, where visitors can learn about the island's history, traditional fishing techniques, and the importance

of marine conservation. These exhibitions often feature local crafts, photographs, and historical artifacts related to the sea.
- **Community Gatherings:** The Festival of the Sea is a time for the community to come together and celebrate their shared heritage. The festival concludes with a large communal meal, featuring fresh seafood and other local dishes, symbolizing the island's connection to the sea and the importance of community.

Annual Events and Festivals in Lipari

Lipari is a vibrant destination where cultural traditions and community spirit are celebrated throughout the year. The island's annual events and festivals offer visitors a chance to immerse themselves in local culture, experience time-honored customs, and enjoy the lively atmosphere that characterizes Lipari's social calendar.

1. Feast of San Bartolomeo (Festa di San Bartolomeo)

Date: August 24th
Significance: The Feast of San Bartolomeo is the most important religious festival on Lipari, dedicated to the island's patron saint, Saint Bartholomew. This festival is a deeply rooted tradition that combines religious devotion with community celebration.

Key Events:

- **Religious Procession:** The centerpiece of the festival is the solemn procession in which a statue of San Bartolomeo is carried through the streets of Lipari. The procession starts at the Cathedral of San Bartolomeo, with locals and visitors alike joining in the procession, accompanied by prayers, hymns, and music.
- **Mass and Blessing:** A special mass is held at the cathedral, followed by the blessing of the waters, a ritual that reflects Lipari's connection to the sea.
- **Festivities:** The religious observances are followed by a lively celebration featuring music, dancing, street performances, and a grand fireworks display over the harbor, illuminating the night sky and creating a magical atmosphere.

Cultural Experience: The Feast of San Bartolomeo is not just a religious event but also a cultural celebration that brings the community together. Visitors are welcomed to participate, offering a unique opportunity to experience the island's traditions and hospitality.

2. Carnival of Lipari (Carnevale di Lipari)

Date: February or March (dates vary depending on Lent)
Significance: Carnival in Lipari is a time of vibrant celebration, marked by colorful parades, elaborate costumes, and joyous festivities that lead up to the period of Lent.

Key Events:

- **Grand Parade:** The highlight of the Carnival is the grand parade, where participants dress in extravagant costumes

and masks, often inspired by historical, mythical, or humorous themes. The parade moves through the streets of Lipari, accompanied by lively music, dancing, and street performances.
- **Children's Carnival:** Special events are organized for children, including costume contests, games, and activities that allow the younger generation to partake in the festivities.
- **Feasting and Parties:** Carnival is also a time for indulging in delicious food and drink before the fasting period of Lent. Many local eateries and homes host special feasts featuring traditional dishes and sweets associated with the Carnival season.

Cultural Experience: Carnival in Lipari is a festive time that showcases the island's creativity and community spirit. The joyous atmosphere is infectious, making it an ideal time for visitors to experience the island's vibrant culture.

3. Aeolian Film Festival

Date: June or July (dates vary)
Significance: The Aeolian Film Festival is an international event that celebrates cinema, particularly films that focus on themes related to the sea, islands, and the environment. It is a key cultural event on Lipari's calendar, attracting filmmakers, critics, and film enthusiasts from around the world.

Key Events:
- **Film Screenings:** The festival features outdoor film screenings in picturesque locations across the island, allowing audiences to enjoy movies under the stars. The

selection includes a mix of international, independent, and documentary films.
- **Workshops and Panels:** The festival hosts workshops, panel discussions, and Q&A sessions with filmmakers, providing insights into the creative process and the themes explored in the films.
- **Awards Ceremony:** The festival concludes with an awards ceremony, recognizing outstanding films and filmmakers. Categories often include Best Feature Film, Best Documentary, and Audience Choice Award.

Cultural Experience: The Aeolian Film Festival offers a unique cultural experience, blending the magic of cinema with the natural beauty of Lipari. It's an opportunity to engage with thought-provoking films while enjoying the island's stunning landscapes.

4. Malvasia Wine Festival

Date: Late August or Early September
Significance: The Malvasia Wine Festival is a celebration of Lipari's most famous wine, Malvasia delle Lipari. This festival highlights the island's rich winemaking tradition and provides an opportunity for visitors to taste and learn about this unique wine.

Key Events:

- **Wine Tastings:** The festival features wine tastings at various locations across the island, where visitors can sample different varieties of Malvasia, including the sweet Passito and dry versions. Local winemakers share their knowledge and passion for the craft, offering insights into the winemaking process.

- **Cultural Events:** In addition to tastings, the festival includes cultural events such as music performances, art exhibitions, and traditional dances that celebrate the island's heritage.
- **Gastronomic Delights:** The festival is also a showcase for local cuisine, with food stalls offering traditional Aeolian dishes that pair perfectly with the wines.

Cultural Experience: The Malvasia Wine Festival is a delightful celebration of Lipari's culinary and viticultural traditions. It's a time to savor the flavors of the island and experience its warm hospitality.

5. Festival of the Sea (Festa del Mare)

Date: July

Significance: The Festival of the Sea honors Lipari's deep connection to the sea, which has shaped the island's culture, economy, and way of life. This festival celebrates the maritime traditions of the Aeolian Islands with a variety of events and activities.

Key Events:

- **Boat Races:** One of the main attractions of the festival is the boat races, where local fishermen and sailors compete in traditional and modern boats. These races are a nod to the island's seafaring heritage.
- **Fishing Competitions:** The festival includes fishing competitions that showcase the skills and techniques passed down through generations. These events are both competitive and educational, highlighting the importance of sustainable fishing practices.

- **Seafood Feasts:** No Festival of the Sea would be complete without a feast, and Lipari delivers with a seafood extravaganza. Freshly caught fish, shellfish, and other marine delicacies are prepared and served at communal tables, bringing together locals and visitors for a shared meal.

Cultural Experience: The Festival of the Sea is a lively and engaging event that celebrates Lipari's maritime heritage. It's an ideal time to experience the island's strong sense of community and its enduring relationship with the sea.

6. Holy Week and Easter Celebrations (Settimana Santa e Pasqua)

Date: March or April (dates vary)
Significance: Holy Week and Easter are important religious observances in Lipari, marked by a series of solemn and moving events that reflect the island's deep Catholic faith.

Key Events:

- **Processions:** Holy Week features several processions, including the Procession of the Dead Christ on Good Friday, where a statue of the crucified Christ is carried through the streets, followed by mourners. The procession is accompanied by prayers, hymns, and the tolling of church bells.
- **Easter Vigil:** The Easter Vigil on Holy Saturday is a significant event, with a midnight mass celebrating the resurrection of Christ. Churches across the island are filled with worshippers, and the service is followed by a joyful celebration.

- **Easter Sunday:** On Easter Sunday, the island comes alive with joy and festivity. Families gather for special meals, and the streets are filled with people celebrating the resurrection. Traditional Easter dishes, such as lamb and sweet pastries, are enjoyed, and the day is marked by a sense of renewal and hope.

Cultural Experience: Holy Week and Easter in Lipari offer a profound spiritual and cultural experience. The events are deeply rooted in tradition and provide an opportunity to witness the island's religious devotion.

Local Customs and Traditions in Lipari: A Glimpse into Island Life

Lipari is a place where ancient customs and traditions are still very much alive, offering a unique cultural experience for visitors. The island's local customs are deeply rooted in its history, religious beliefs, and seafaring heritage. Engaging with these traditions provides a deeper understanding of the island's way of life and offers an enriching cultural experience.

1. Religious Devotion and Practices

Faith at the Core:

Religion plays a central role in the lives of Lipari's residents, with Catholicism being the dominant faith. The island is dotted with churches and chapels, each serving as a focal point for the community's spiritual life. The Church of San Bartolomeo, dedicated to the island's patron saint, is particularly significant.

Festivals and Processions: Religious festivals, especially those honoring saints, are a vital part of life in Lipari. These events often involve elaborate processions where statues of saints are carried through the streets, accompanied by prayers, hymns, and music. The Feast of San Bartolomeo, celebrated on August 24th, is the most important religious festival, attracting locals and visitors alike.

Daily Rituals: Many locals still observe traditional daily rituals, such as attending mass, lighting candles in churches, and saying prayers at home. These practices reflect the island's deep spiritual connection and the importance of faith in everyday life.

2. Family and Community Values

Strong Family Bonds: Family is the cornerstone of social life in Lipari. Extended families often live close to one another, and family gatherings are frequent. Meals are a time for families to come together, share stories, and maintain strong bonds. The concept of "la famiglia" (the family) extends beyond the nuclear family, encompassing a wide network of relatives.

Community Spirit: Lipari's sense of community is strong, with a deep-rooted tradition of mutual support and cooperation. Neighbors look out for one another, and community events are well-attended. This communal spirit is particularly evident during festivals, religious ceremonies, and public celebrations, where everyone comes together to participate and contribute.

Respect for Elders: Respect for elders is a fundamental value in Lipari's culture. Older generations are revered for their wisdom and experience, and their opinions are highly valued within the family and community. It is common for younger people to care for their elderly relatives, ensuring they are well-supported in their later years.

3. Traditional Crafts and Artisanry

Ceramics and Pottery: Lipari has a long tradition of ceramics and pottery, dating back to ancient times. The island's artisans are skilled in creating a variety of ceramic items, from decorative tiles and vases to functional kitchenware. These handmade products often feature traditional designs and motifs that have been passed down through generations.

Textiles and Embroidery: Embroidery and textile work are also significant aspects of Lipari's artisan tradition. Local women often create intricate embroidery, lace, and woven textiles that are used in both everyday life and special occasions. These crafts are typically learned from older family members, ensuring the continuation of these skills.

Jewelry and Coral Work: The art of jewelry-making, particularly using coral and other local materials, is another important craft in Lipari. Coral jewelry, in particular, is a specialty of the Aeolian Islands, with artisans creating beautiful pieces that reflect the island's connection to the sea.

4. Traditional Music and Dance

Folk Music: Traditional Aeolian music, characterized by its lively rhythms and soulful melodies, is an integral part of Lipari's cultural heritage. Folk songs often tell stories of the sea, love, and daily life, and are typically accompanied by instruments such as the tambourine, accordion, and guitar.

Taranta Dance: The "taranta" is a traditional dance of the Aeolian Islands, known for its energetic and rhythmic movements. It is usually performed during festivals and celebrations, with dancers following the rhythm of folk music. The dance is a communal activity, with people of all ages joining in, creating a joyful and inclusive atmosphere.

Festive Performances: During major festivals, such as Carnival and the Feast of San Bartolomeo, music and dance are central to the celebrations. These performances are a way for the community to express their cultural identity and to pass on traditions to younger generations.

5. Culinary Traditions

Family Recipes: Culinary traditions in Lipari are closely tied to family and community. Recipes are often passed down through generations, with each family adding its own twist to traditional dishes. Meals are a time for gathering, with food playing a central role in social interactions.

Seasonal and Local Ingredients: The island's cuisine is based on fresh, local ingredients, with a strong emphasis on seafood, vegetables, and herbs. Seasonal eating is a key aspect of Lipari's culinary tradition, with dishes varying according to what is available throughout the year.

Food as Celebration: Food is an essential part of any celebration in Lipari. Special dishes are prepared for religious festivals, weddings, and other significant events, often involving communal cooking and sharing of food. Traditional dishes such as "caponata" (a vegetable dish), "pane cunzato" (seasoned bread), and "malvasia" (a sweet wine) are staples at these gatherings.

6. Maritime Traditions

Fishing Practices: Lipari's maritime traditions are deeply ingrained in its culture. Fishing has been a way of life for centuries, and many of the island's customs revolve around the sea. Traditional fishing techniques, such as using nets and traps, are still practiced by local fishermen.

Boat Building: Boat building is another important tradition, with local craftsmen skilled in constructing traditional wooden boats known as "gozzi." These boats are used for fishing, transportation, and festivals, where they are often decorated and paraded along the coast.

Blessing of the Boats: An important maritime tradition is the annual blessing of the boats, which takes place during the Festival of the Sea. This ritual involves priests blessing the fishing boats and the waters, praying for a safe and bountiful fishing season. The event is accompanied by a procession and a communal meal, celebrating the island's seafaring heritage.

7. Celebrating Life Events

Weddings: Weddings in Lipari are grand celebrations that often involve the entire community. Traditional weddings include a church ceremony followed by a large reception with food, music, and dancing. The bride and groom are often serenaded with traditional songs, and the celebrations can last well into the night.

Baptisms and First Communions: Baptisms and first communions are important religious milestones that are celebrated with family gatherings and feasts. These events are marked by special church services, followed by communal meals and the giving of gifts.

Funerals: Funerals in Lipari are solemn occasions that reflect the island's deep religious beliefs. The entire community often participates in the funeral processions, paying their respects to the deceased and offering support to the grieving family. Traditional mourning practices, such as wearing black and observing a period of mourning, are still observed.

Overall, these customs are not just remnants of the past; they are a living part of the island's identity, connecting the present to its rich heritage. For visitors, engaging with these traditions offers a deeper connection to the island and its people, making a visit to Lipari truly unforgettable.

SHOPPING OPTIONS

Shopping in Lipari is an experience that goes beyond the usual tourist souvenirs. The island offers a delightful array of local products, from handcrafted goods to regional delicacies, making it a perfect place to discover unique items that reflect the island's rich culture and heritage. Are you looking for a special memento of your visit or gifts to bring back home, the shops and markets in Lipari are brimming with authentic and distinctive treasures.

1. Local Artisans and Handcrafted Goods

Ceramics and Pottery: Lipari is renowned for its beautiful ceramic pieces, which are often handmade by local artisans. These items range from decorative tiles and vases to practical kitchenware, all featuring vibrant colors and intricate designs inspired by the island's natural beauty and historical motifs. Purchasing a piece of Lipari pottery is like taking home a piece of the island's artistic soul.

Jewelry
Another popular item to shop for in Lipari is handmade jewelry. Local artisans craft stunning pieces using materials like coral, lava stone, and shells, often incorporating traditional Aeolian symbols and designs. These unique accessories make for meaningful keepsakes or gifts that carry the essence of the island.

Textiles and Embroidery: The island is also known for its exquisite textiles, including handwoven fabrics and embroidered linens. These items, often crafted using traditional techniques passed down through generations, include tablecloths, napkins, and clothing items adorned with intricate patterns. They not only serve as functional pieces but also as beautiful reminders of Lipari's cultural heritage.

2. Gourmet Food Products

Eolian Delicacies: Lipari offers a variety of gourmet food products that are perfect for food lovers. Local specialties include capers, olives, and sun-dried tomatoes, which are often sold in small, family-run shops. These ingredients, known for their intense flavors, are staples of the Aeolian cuisine and make excellent gifts for anyone who enjoys cooking.

Local Wines: Wine enthusiasts will find a selection of local wines made from grapes grown in the island's volcanic soil. The unique terroir of Lipari gives these wines a distinct flavor profile, making them a must-try for visitors. Bottles of Malvasia, a sweet dessert wine, and other regional varieties are widely available in local wine shops and make for an excellent souvenir of your trip.

Pastries and Sweets: Don't miss out on the island's traditional sweets and pastries, which can be found in local bakeries and specialty food stores. Treats like "cannoli" filled with sweet ricotta or "cassata" made with marzipan and sponge cake are local favorites. These delicious items are perfect for sampling during your stay or for taking home as a sweet reminder of Lipari.

3. Shopping Districts and Markets

Main Shopping Streets: The heart of Lipari's shopping scene is found in the main streets of the town center, particularly along Corso Vittorio Emanuele. Here, you'll find a mix of boutiques, artisan shops, and specialty stores offering everything from fashion and accessories to home decor and souvenirs. Strolling through these vibrant streets is a pleasure in itself, with the added bonus of discovering unique items at every turn.

Local Markets: For a more authentic shopping experience, visit one of Lipari's local markets. These markets are a great place to find fresh produce, local cheeses, and other regional products. The bustling atmosphere, combined with the chance to interact with local vendors, makes shopping at these markets a memorable part of any visit to Lipari.

4. Shopping Tips and Etiquette

Bargaining: While many of the shops in Lipari have fixed prices, particularly for artisan goods and specialty items, there may be some room for polite negotiation in markets or smaller, family-run stores. However, it's important to be respectful when bargaining, and always approach it with a friendly attitude.

Supporting Local Businesses: When shopping in Lipari, consider supporting local artisans and small businesses. Not only do you get to take home unique, high-quality products, but you also contribute to the local economy and help preserve the island's cultural traditions.

Packaging and Shipping: If you're purchasing larger items or fragile goods like ceramics or wine, ask the shop if they offer packaging or shipping services. Many stores in Lipari are accustomed to catering to tourists and may provide options to ship your purchases home, ensuring they arrive safely.

Souvenirs and Local Crafts in Lipari

Lipari, offers a wide array of souvenirs and local crafts that capture the essence of the island. It doesn't matter you're looking for a memento of your travels or a gift for someone back home, Lipari's markets, artisan shops, and boutiques are filled with unique items that reflect the island's heritage.

1. Handmade Ceramics: Art Inspired by Tradition

Traditional Pottery: One of the most iconic souvenirs from Lipari is its handmade ceramics. The island has a long-standing tradition of pottery, with local artisans crafting everything from decorative tiles to functional kitchenware. These ceramics often feature bright, bold colors and intricate patterns inspired by the Mediterranean landscape and ancient Aeolian culture. Plates, bowls, and vases adorned with marine motifs, floral designs, or geometric shapes make beautiful keepsakes that are both practical and artistic.

Tiles and Wall Art: In addition to pottery, ceramic tiles are popular souvenirs that showcase the island's artistic flair. These tiles, which often depict scenes of Lipari's picturesque landscapes or traditional symbols, can be used as decorative wall art or coasters. They serve as a beautiful reminder of your time on the island and are easy to pack for travel.

2. Local Jewelry: Adornments with a Story

Coral and Lava Stone Jewelry: Lipari's proximity to the sea and its volcanic origins are reflected in the unique jewelry made from coral and lava stone. Coral jewelry, which ranges from simple necklaces to elaborate bracelets, is prized for its natural beauty and connection to the island's maritime culture. Lava stone, with its dark, porous texture, is often paired with other materials to create striking pieces that are both modern and rooted in tradition.

Shell and Sea Glass Creations: Another popular form of jewelry in Lipari is made from shells and sea glass. These materials, naturally shaped and smoothed by the sea, are often crafted into necklaces, earrings, and bracelets that carry the essence of the island's coastal charm. These pieces are perfect for those who want a souvenir that reflects Lipari's natural beauty.

3. Textiles and Embroidery: A Touch of Handmade Elegance

Handwoven Fabrics: Lipari's textile tradition is another treasure trove for visitors. Local artisans create handwoven fabrics that are used to make a variety of products, from scarves and shawls to tablecloths and throws. These items, often made from natural fibers like cotton and linen, feature intricate patterns and vibrant colors that echo the island's landscapes. A handwoven textile from Lipari is not only a beautiful souvenir but also a testament to the island's artisanal craftsmanship.

Embroidered Linens: Embroidered linens are another specialty of Lipari. These finely crafted items, which include napkins, table runners, and pillowcases, are often adorned with traditional Aeolian designs and motifs. The attention to detail and the quality of the embroidery make these linens a cherished keepsake that adds a touch of Lipari's elegance to your home.

4. Artistic Keepsakes: Paintings and Photography

Local Artworks: For those who appreciate fine art, Lipari offers a selection of local paintings and prints that depict the island's stunning landscapes and seascapes. These artworks, created by local artists, often capture the vibrant colors and serene beauty of Lipari, making them a perfect addition to your home decor.

Photography Prints: Photography enthusiasts can also find beautiful prints of Lipari's iconic views, from the dramatic cliffs to the charming villages. These high-quality prints are often available in galleries and souvenir shops and serve as a lasting memory of the island's breathtaking scenery.

5. Aromatic Souvenirs: Perfumes and Soaps

Handmade Soaps and Perfumes: Lipari's natural environment provides the inspiration for a range of handmade soaps and perfumes. These products, often made with local ingredients like olive oil, lavender, and citrus, capture the essence of the island's aromatic landscape. Handmade soaps, with their natural scents and gentle ingredients, make a thoughtful and practical gift. Similarly, locally produced perfumes offer a sensory reminder of your time in Lipari, with fragrances that evoke the island's fresh sea breeze and blooming flowers.

Herbal Sachets and Essential Oils: Another aromatic souvenir from Lipari includes herbal sachets and essential oils made from locally grown plants. These items are perfect for bringing a piece of Lipari's natural scent into your home. Herbal sachets, filled with lavender or other fragrant herbs, can be used to freshen up closets or drawers, while essential oils are ideal for aromatherapy.

6. Supporting Local Artisans and Sustainable Shopping

Ethical Purchases: When shopping for souvenirs in Lipari, consider purchasing from local artisans and small businesses. Not only does this support the local economy, but it also ensures that you're buying authentic products that are crafted with care and respect for the island's traditions.

Sustainable Souvenirs: Opt for souvenirs that are environmentally friendly and sustainably sourced. Handmade products, especially those using natural materials or traditional methods, often have a lower environmental impact compared to mass-produced items. Additionally, many local artisans in Lipari are committed to sustainable practices, making your purchase even more meaningful.

Best Shopping Streets and Markets in Lipari: Where to Find the Perfect Souvenirs

1. Corso Vittorio Emanuele

Corso Vittorio Emanuele is the main shopping thoroughfare in Lipari town and the epicenter of the island's commercial activity. This bustling street is lined with a variety of shops, from chic boutiques to traditional artisan stores, making it the perfect place to start your shopping adventure. The atmosphere here is lively and vibrant, with a mix of locals and tourists enjoying the charm of the old town.

What You'll Find

- **Artisan Boutiques**: Along Corso Vittorio Emanuele, you'll discover a wide range of artisan boutiques selling handmade jewelry, ceramics, and textiles. These shops often feature items crafted by local artists, making each piece unique and reflective of the island's cultural identity.
- **Fashion and Accessories**: Fashion enthusiasts will find an array of boutiques offering stylish clothing and accessories. Whether you're looking for Mediterranean-inspired outfits or unique accessories made from local materials like coral and lava stone, this street has something for every taste.
- **Gourmet Food Shops**: The street is also home to several gourmet food shops where you can purchase local delicacies such as capers, olive oil, and wines. These items make for excellent souvenirs that allow you to take a taste of Lipari back home.

Tips for Shoppers

- **Explore Side Streets**: Don't just stick to the main thoroughfare—venture into the side streets branching off Corso Vittorio Emanuele, where you can find hidden gems and less crowded shops.
- **Shop for Local Crafts**: Look for shops that specifically highlight local crafts and products. These items are not only unique but also support the local economy and artisans.

2. Piazza di Marina Corta

Piazza di Marina Corta is a charming square located near the waterfront, offering a picturesque setting for shopping. This area is known for its relaxed ambiance and beautiful views of the harbor, making it a favorite spot for both locals and visitors. The square is surrounded by a variety of shops, cafes, and restaurants, creating a perfect blend of shopping and leisure.

What You'll Find

- **Souvenir Shops**: The square is dotted with small souvenir shops where you can find everything from postcards and magnets to more elaborate items like handmade pottery and glassware.
- **Art Galleries**: For art lovers, the square is home to a few galleries that showcase works by local artists. These galleries often feature paintings, sculptures, and photography that depict the stunning landscapes and seascapes of Lipari.
- **Local Markets**: During the summer months, Piazza di Marina Corta often hosts small markets where local

vendors sell a variety of goods, including fresh produce, handmade crafts, and traditional Aeolian products.

Tips for Shoppers

- **Visit in the Evening**: The square comes alive in the evening, with street vendors setting up stalls and locals gathering for a leisurely stroll. It's a great time to shop and soak in the local atmosphere.
- **Enjoy a Coffee Break**: Take a break from shopping and enjoy a coffee or gelato at one of the cafes in the square. The views of the harbor and surrounding area are particularly beautiful at sunset.

3. Via Garibaldi

Via Garibaldi is another prominent shopping street in Lipari, offering a mix of traditional shops and modern boutiques. This street, located near the historic center, is slightly quieter than Corso Vittorio Emanuele, making it ideal for those who prefer a more relaxed shopping experience.

What You'll Find

- **Craft Stores**: Via Garibaldi is known for its craft stores, where you can find a variety of handmade goods, including ceramics, textiles, and jewelry. These shops often carry items that are inspired by the island's natural beauty and cultural heritage.
- **Specialty Shops**: Along Via Garibaldi, you'll also find specialty shops that focus on particular types of products, such as gourmet foods, wines, or olive oil. These stores are perfect for picking up high-quality, locally produced items.

- **Fashion Boutiques**: The street features several fashion boutiques offering a mix of local designs and popular Italian brands. Whether you're looking for a new outfit or a unique accessory, you're likely to find something special here.

Tips for Shoppers

- **Engage with Shop Owners**: Many of the shops on Via Garibaldi are family-run businesses, and the owners are often happy to share the stories behind their products. Engaging with them can enhance your shopping experience and give you a deeper appreciation for the items you purchase.
- **Take Your Time**: Via Garibaldi is less crowded than some of the other shopping areas, so take your time to browse and explore the different stores at your own pace.

4. Lipari's Local Markets

For an authentic taste of local life, visiting one of Lipari's markets is a must. These markets offer a vibrant mix of fresh produce, artisanal products, and handmade crafts, providing a true reflection of the island's culture and traditions.

What You'll Find

- **Farmers' Markets**: Lipari's farmers' markets are the best place to find fresh fruits, vegetables, and other locally grown produce. These markets often feature seasonal items, including the island's famous capers and tomatoes, as well as freshly caught seafood.

- **Craft Markets**: During the tourist season, Lipari hosts craft markets where local artisans sell their handmade goods. From jewelry and ceramics to textiles and leatherwork, these markets are a treasure trove of unique items that you won't find anywhere else.
- **Food Markets**: Lipari's food markets are a haven for food lovers. Here, you can purchase local delicacies like cheeses, cured meats, olive oil, and honey, as well as sample some of the island's traditional dishes.

Tips for Shoppers

- **Arrive Early**: For the best selection, especially at farmers' markets, it's a good idea to arrive early. This is also when the markets are less crowded, allowing for a more leisurely shopping experience.
- **Bring Cash**: While some vendors may accept credit cards, it's advisable to bring cash, as smaller stalls and markets may not have card payment facilities.
- **Ask for Recommendations**: Don't hesitate to ask vendors for their recommendations, whether you're looking for the freshest produce or the best local cheese. They often have insider tips on the best products to try.

5. Specialty Stores and Hidden Gems

Beyond the main shopping streets and markets, Lipari is home to a number of specialty stores and hidden gems that offer unique shopping experiences. These stores are often located off the beaten path but are well worth seeking out.

What You'll Find

- **Antique Shops**: Lipari has a few antique shops where you can find vintage items, including furniture, jewelry, and decorative pieces. These stores offer a glimpse into the island's past and are perfect for those who appreciate history and craftsmanship.
- **Gourmet Food and Wine Stores**: If you're looking for high-quality gourmet products, there are several specialty stores in Lipari that focus on local delicacies and wines. These stores often carry rare items and are a great place to find something truly special.
- **Artisan Workshops**: Some of Lipari's artisans open their workshops to the public, allowing you to see the crafting process firsthand. These workshops often double as stores, where you can purchase one-of-a-kind items directly from the maker.

Tips for Shoppers

- **Explore Beyond the Main Streets**: Some of the best shopping experiences in Lipari can be found by venturing off the main streets and exploring the less touristy areas. Keep an eye out for small, unassuming shops that may hold hidden treasures.
- **Support Local Artisans**: By purchasing directly from artisans and small businesses, you're supporting the local economy and helping to preserve Lipari's cultural heritage.

Art Galleries and Boutiques in Lipari

The island boasts a variety of art galleries and boutiques that showcase the work of local artists and artisans. These spaces provide visitors with the opportunity to explore and purchase unique artworks and handcrafted items that reflect Lipari's rich heritage.

Galleria d'Arte Lipari

Galleria d'Arte Lipari is a prominent gallery located in the heart of Lipari's historic center. This gallery features a rotating collection of artworks by both local and regional artists, including paintings, sculptures, and mixed-media pieces. The gallery aims to promote the island's artistic heritage while also offering a platform for contemporary artists.

What You'll Find

- **Paintings and Prints**: The gallery showcases a range of paintings and prints that capture the beauty of Lipari's landscapes and seascapes. You'll find works that range from traditional depictions of the island to modern interpretations of its natural beauty.
- **Sculptures**: The gallery often exhibits sculptures made from various materials, including local stone and wood. These pieces reflect the island's artistic diversity and provide a three-dimensional perspective on its cultural themes.
- **Exhibitions and Events**: Galleria d'Arte Lipari regularly hosts exhibitions, artist talks, and workshops. Check their schedule for special events that offer deeper insights into the local art scene and opportunities to interact with artists.

Tips for Visitors

- **Check Exhibition Schedules**: Before visiting, check the gallery's website or contact them to find out about current and upcoming exhibitions.

- **Purchase Art**: The gallery provides opportunities to purchase original artworks, making it a great place to find a unique and meaningful souvenir.

Art Gallery Marina Corta

Located near the charming Piazza di Marina Corta, Art Gallery Marina Corta specializes in artworks that capture the essence of Lipari and the surrounding Aeolian Islands. This gallery features a variety of artistic styles and mediums, offering a diverse selection of pieces for art enthusiasts.

What You'll Find

- **Local Landscapes**: Many artworks focus on the stunning landscapes and seascapes of the Aeolian Islands, providing a visual representation of the region's natural beauty.
- **Traditional and Modern Art**: The gallery showcases a mix of traditional and contemporary art, offering something for every taste. You'll find everything from classic paintings to innovative modern pieces.
- **Crafts and Prints**: In addition to original artworks, the gallery often features prints and smaller crafts that make for excellent gifts or souvenirs.

Tips for Visitors

- **Explore the Area**: After visiting the gallery, take a stroll around Piazza di Marina Corta to enjoy the picturesque views and vibrant atmosphere.
- **Support Local Artists**: Consider purchasing a piece of art to support local talent and take home a unique memory of your visit.

Boutiques

Boutique Eoliana is a well-regarded shop that specializes in high-quality, handcrafted items reflecting the island's unique cultural heritage. Located on Corso Vittorio Emanuele, this boutique offers a range of artisanal products, from textiles to jewelry, all made with attention to detail and traditional techniques.

What You'll Find

- **Handmade Jewelry**: The boutique features a stunning selection of jewelry made from local materials such as coral, lava stone, and shells. These pieces are designed to highlight the natural beauty and craftsmanship of the Aeolian Islands.
- **Textiles**: Boutique Eoliana offers handwoven fabrics, including scarves, shawls, and table linens. These items often feature traditional patterns and vibrant colors inspired by the island's landscapes.
- **Home Decor**: You'll also find a range of home decor items, including ceramics, decorative tiles, and artwork. Each piece is crafted to reflect the island's aesthetic and cultural traditions.

Tips for Visitors

- **Explore the Full Range**: Take your time to browse the boutique's diverse selection of items, as each piece is unique and reflects the island's artisanal traditions.
- **Ask About Custom Orders**: Some boutiques may offer custom orders or bespoke items. Inquire if you're interested in a specific design or piece that can be tailored to your preferences.

L'Arte della Ceramica

L'Arte della Ceramica is a boutique dedicated to showcasing the island's rich ceramic traditions. Located in the historic center of Lipari, this shop offers a wide range of handcrafted ceramics, from decorative tiles to functional tableware.

What You'll Find

- **Decorative Ceramics**: The boutique features a variety of decorative ceramics, including tiles and wall art that depict scenes of Lipari's landscapes and cultural motifs.
- **Tableware**: You can also find practical yet beautifully designed tableware, such as plates, bowls, and pitchers. Each piece is handmade and often features intricate designs that celebrate the island's heritage.
- **Custom Pieces**: L'Arte della Ceramica offers the option to order custom ceramic pieces, allowing you to create a personalized souvenir that captures the essence of Lipari.

Tips for Visitors

- **Inspect the Craftsmanship**: Take a close look at the craftsmanship of the ceramics, as each piece is made with care and attention to detail.
- **Consider Shipping Options**: If you purchase larger or more delicate items, inquire about shipping options to ensure your souvenirs arrive home safely.

Hidden Gems: Unique Finds and Local Treasures

Mercato dell'Arte

Mercato dell'Arte is a small, charming market located near Piazza di Marina Corta that features a selection of local crafts and artworks. This market is an excellent place to discover unique and handmade items that reflect the island's artistic spirit.

What You'll Find

- **Local Crafts**: The market offers a variety of crafts, including pottery, jewelry, and textiles made by local artisans. Each item is a testament to the island's traditional skills and creative flair.
- **Artisanal Goods**: You can also find artisanal goods such as handmade soaps, perfumes, and other products that highlight the island's natural resources and local expertise.
- **Artwork**: Some local artists set up stalls at the market to sell their paintings, prints, and other artworks. This is a great opportunity to purchase original pieces directly from the artist.

Tips for Visitors

- **Visit During Market Days**: Check the market schedule to visit during active market days, when there is a wider selection of items and a more vibrant atmosphere.
- **Interact with Vendors**: Engage with the vendors to learn more about their crafts and the inspiration behind their work. This interaction can enhance your shopping experience and provide valuable insights into the island's artistic community.

Bottega dei Fiori

Bottega dei Fiori is a boutique known for its floral-themed crafts and decorative items. Located in a quaint corner of Lipari, this shop offers a range of handcrafted products inspired by the island's natural beauty.

What You'll Find

- **Floral Decorations**: The boutique specializes in floral-themed decorations, including paintings, ceramics, and textiles. These items often feature designs inspired by the island's flora and picturesque landscapes.
- **Crafted Gifts**: You can find a variety of handcrafted gifts, such as scented sachets, soaps, and candles, all featuring floral motifs that capture the essence of Lipari's natural environment.
- **Unique Keepsakes**: The shop also offers unique keepsakes like handmade cards and prints, making it a great place to find a special gift or memento.

Tips for Visitors

- **Explore the Craftsmanship**: Pay attention to the detailed craftsmanship of the floral-themed items, as each piece is designed to capture the island's beauty.
- **Consider Seasonal Items**: Depending on the time of year, the boutique may offer seasonal items or limited-edition products that make for unique souvenirs.

DAY TRIPS AND EXCURSIONS: EXPLORING BEYOND LIPARI

Lipari offers more than just its own stunning landscapes and cultural treasures. The island's strategic location makes it an ideal starting point for a range of day trips and excursions to nearby islands and attractions. These excursions allow visitors to experience the diverse beauty and unique characteristics of the Aeolian archipelago. Here are some of the best day trips and excursions you can take from Lipari.

Vulcano Island

Vulcano Island, one of the Aeolian Islands, is a place of rugged beauty, where the power of nature is evident in every corner. Known for its volcanic activity, therapeutic mud baths, and dramatic landscapes, Vulcano offers a unique experience for those visiting the Aeolian archipelago. Here's everything you need to know about exploring this fascinating island.

Getting to Vulcano Island

By Ferry: Vulcano Island is easily accessible from Lipari by ferry, with several daily departures that make the short journey of around 10-20 minutes. Ferries are operated by different companies, and schedules can vary depending on the season. During peak season, it's advisable to book tickets in advance to secure your spot.

By Private Boat: For a more personalized trip, you can hire a private boat from Lipari. This option allows you to enjoy a scenic and flexible journey, taking in the stunning views of the Aeolian Islands as you approach Vulcano.

By Organized Tour: Numerous organized tours from Lipari include Vulcano as a key stop. These tours often combine visits to multiple islands, providing a convenient way to explore Vulcano along with other nearby destinations.

Top Attractions on Vulcano Island

1. Gran Cratere (Great Crater)

The Gran Cratere is the most iconic feature of Vulcano Island, offering a thrilling experience for visitors. The hike to the top of this still-active volcano is moderately challenging but incredibly rewarding, with panoramic views that stretch across the Aeolian Islands.

- **The Hike**: The ascent to the crater takes about 1-1.5 hours, depending on your pace. The trail is well-marked but can be steep and rocky in places. The sight of fumaroles emitting sulfurous steam and the barren, moon-like landscape at the summit makes the effort worthwhile.
- **What to Bring**: Sturdy hiking shoes are essential, as is plenty of water and a hat to protect from the sun. The smell of sulfur is strong near the crater, so those sensitive to strong odors might want to bring a mask.

2. Mud Baths and Thermal Springs

Vulcano is famous for its natural mud baths, known for their therapeutic properties. Located near Porto di Levante, the mud baths are rich in minerals and are believed to benefit the skin and joints.

- **Thermal Mud Baths**: The experience involves covering your body in warm, sulfur-rich mud, letting it dry in the

sun, and then rinsing off in the nearby sea. The process is said to detoxify and rejuvenate the skin.
- **Tips for Visitors**: Bring an old swimsuit that you don't mind getting stained, as the sulfur can leave a lasting odor. It's also a good idea to rinse thoroughly after the bath and avoid wearing jewelry that could be tarnished by the sulfur.

3. Spiaggia delle Sabbie Nere (Black Sand Beach)

One of Vulcano's most popular beaches, Spiaggia delle Sabbie Nere, is known for its unique black sand, the result of volcanic activity. The contrast between the dark sand and the clear blue waters creates a striking visual experience.

- **Beach Activities**: The calm waters make this beach perfect for swimming and snorkeling. There are also sun loungers and umbrellas available for rent, making it a great spot to relax and soak up the sun.
- **Nearby Amenities**: The beach is close to several bars and restaurants, where you can enjoy a refreshing drink or a meal after a day in the sun.

4. Vulcanello Peninsula

The Vulcanello Peninsula is another volcanic formation on the island, offering beautiful views and fascinating geological features. The area is home to a series of lava formations and offers some of the best vantage points on the island.

- **Scenic Walks**: The trails around Vulcanello provide stunning views of the surrounding islands and the smoldering Gran Cratere. The landscape is otherworldly, with solidified lava flows and strange rock formations.

- **Photography Tips**: The golden hours of early morning and late afternoon provide the best lighting for capturing the rugged beauty of Vulcanello.

Dining and Refreshments

After exploring the island, indulge in some local cuisine at one of Vulcano's restaurants. The island's culinary offerings include fresh seafood, traditional Aeolian dishes, and refreshing granitas.

- **Local Specialties**: Try dishes like spaghetti alla vulcanara, a pasta dish with capers, olives, and fresh tomatoes, or enjoy grilled seafood straight from the Mediterranean.
- **Where to Eat**: Popular dining spots include **Ristorante La Forgia**, known for its seafood, and **Il Castello**, which offers stunning views along with traditional dishes.

Practical Information

Best Time to Visit

- **Spring and Fall**: These seasons are perfect for visiting Vulcano, offering milder temperatures and fewer tourists. The weather is ideal for hiking, exploring, and enjoying the natural thermal baths.
- **Summer**: If you prefer warmer weather and don't mind the crowds, summer is the busiest time on Vulcano, with the island's beaches and attractions in full swing.

What to Bring

- **Sun Protection**: With plenty of outdoor activities, bring sunscreen, a hat, and sunglasses to protect yourself from the sun.

- **Comfortable Clothing**: Light, breathable clothing is ideal for the island's warm climate, and sturdy footwear is a must for hiking the crater and exploring rugged areas.

Health and Safety

- **Hydration**: The volcanic landscape can get hot, especially in summer, so carry plenty of water to stay hydrated.
- **Safety Tips**: Be cautious around the crater, as the terrain can be slippery and the fumes from the fumaroles can be strong. Stick to marked paths and follow local guidelines.

Accommodation on Vulcano

While most visitors stay on Lipari and take day trips to Vulcano, there are several accommodation options on the island itself, ranging from small hotels to guesthouses. Staying overnight allows you to experience the island's unique atmosphere after the day-trippers have left.

Vulcano Island, with its unique landscapes and natural wonders, offers a memorable experience for those exploring the Aeolian Islands.

Salina

Salina, the second-largest of the Aeolian Islands, is often called the "Green Island" due to its lush vegetation and verdant landscapes. Known for its stunning natural beauty, rich history, and delicious Malvasia wine, Salina offers a tranquil retreat for travelers seeking a blend of relaxation and adventure. Here's everything you need to know for an unforgettable journey to Salina.

Getting to Salina

By Ferry

- **From Lipari**: Salina is easily accessible from Lipari, with frequent ferry services connecting the two islands. The journey takes about 30 minutes, making it a convenient day trip or a multi-day stay option.
- **From Mainland Sicily**: Ferries also operate from Milazzo and other ports in Sicily, with direct routes to Salina's ports of Santa Marina and Rinella.

By Hydrofoil

- **Fast and Efficient**: Hydrofoils offer a quicker way to reach Salina from various Aeolian Islands and the mainland. The ride is smooth and provides beautiful views of the archipelago.

By Private Boat

- **Customized Travel**: For a more personalized experience, consider renting a private boat. This option allows you to explore at your own pace, with the freedom to stop and enjoy hidden coves and lesser-known spots along the way.

Top Attractions on Salina

1. Monte Fossa delle Felci and Monte dei Porri

- **Hiking the Twin Peaks**: Salina is home to two extinct volcanoes, Monte Fossa delle Felci and Monte dei Porri, which dominate the island's landscape. The hike to the summit of Monte Fossa delle Felci, the highest point in the

Aeolian Islands, is a must for outdoor enthusiasts. The trail is surrounded by lush ferns, chestnut trees, and wildflowers, and the panoramic views from the top are breathtaking.
- **Nature Reserve**: Both peaks are part of a protected nature reserve, ensuring the preservation of the island's unique flora and fauna. Birdwatchers will delight in spotting various species that inhabit the area.

2. Pollara Beach

- **A Scenic Hideaway**: Pollara Beach, located on the western coast of Salina, is famous for its dramatic cliffs and crystal-clear waters. It's a secluded spot that gained international fame as the setting for the movie "Il Postino."
- **Swimming and Sunbathing**: The beach is ideal for swimming, with its calm, transparent waters. Sunbathers can relax on the pebbled shore, surrounded by stunning natural beauty.
- **Sunset Views**: Pollara is particularly famous for its sunsets. The sun dipping into the sea, framed by the towering cliffs, is a sight not to be missed.

3. Santa Marina Salina

- **The Island's Main Town**: Santa Marina Salina is the bustling heart of the island, with its charming streets, quaint shops, and lively marina. Stroll along the promenade, enjoy an espresso in a local café, and soak in the island's relaxed atmosphere.

- **Historic Church**: Visit the Church of Santa Marina, a beautiful example of Aeolian religious architecture, where you can appreciate the island's cultural heritage.
- **Shopping and Dining**: Santa Marina offers a variety of shops selling local crafts, souvenirs, and Salina's famous Malvasia wine. There are also numerous restaurants where you can savor traditional Aeolian cuisine.

4. Malfa

- **A Picturesque Village**: Malfa is a quaint village on the northern coast of Salina, known for its vineyards, charming streets, and stunning views of the sea. It's an ideal spot for a leisurely walk or a quiet afternoon.
- **Vineyards and Wine Tasting**: Malfa is at the heart of Salina's wine production. Visit one of the local vineyards to sample Malvasia delle Lipari, a sweet dessert wine that has been produced on the island for centuries.

5. Rinella

- **A Tranquil Harbor Town**: Rinella is a small fishing village on the southern coast of Salina, known for its black sand beach and picturesque harbor. It's a peaceful place to explore, with a slower pace than Santa Marina.
- **Cave Houses**: The area is dotted with unique cave houses, carved into the soft rock, which add to Rinella's charm. These ancient dwellings are a testament to the island's history and the resourcefulness of its inhabitants.

Experiencing Salina's Natural Beauty

1. Nature Trails

- **Exploring on Foot**: Salina's well-maintained nature trails make it a hiker's paradise. Whether you're trekking up Monte Fossa delle Felci or taking a leisurely stroll through the island's vineyards, the views are spectacular.
- **Wildlife and Flora**: The island's diverse ecosystem supports a variety of wildlife, including birds, lizards, and rare plants. The mix of volcanic soil and Mediterranean climate creates a rich tapestry of greenery that's a feast for the eyes.

2. Boat Tours

- **Coastal Exploration**: Discover Salina's stunning coastline by boat. Tours are available that circumnavigate the island, offering the chance to see hidden coves, sea caves, and dramatic cliffs.
- **Snorkeling and Diving**: The clear waters around Salina are perfect for snorkeling and diving. Explore underwater caves, vibrant marine life, and shipwrecks that tell the stories of the island's maritime history.

3. Vineyards and Wine Tasting

- **The Essence of Salina**: Wine is an integral part of Salina's culture, and no visit to the island is complete without sampling its famous Malvasia. Many vineyards offer tours and tastings, where you can learn about the winemaking process and enjoy the fruits of the island's labor.
- **Local Wine Producers**: Visit renowned vineyards such as Tenuta di Castellaro or Fenech for an authentic experience. Pair your wine tasting with local delicacies like capers and sundried tomatoes, which are also produced on the island.

Cultural and Historical Sites

1. Museo Civico

- **Island's History**: Located in Santa Marina, the Museo Civico offers insights into Salina's past, from prehistoric times to its development as a major wine producer. The museum's exhibits include archaeological finds, historical artifacts, and displays on the island's geology and ecology.
- **Cultural Significance**: The museum also showcases the island's cultural heritage, including traditional Aeolian costumes, tools, and crafts.

2. Churches and Religious Sites

- **Cultural Landmarks**: Salina is home to several charming churches, each with its own unique history and architectural style. Visit the Church of San Lorenzo in Malfa or the Church of Maria SS. Addolorata in Leni to experience the island's religious traditions.
- **Festivals**: The island's religious festivals are a highlight for visitors, featuring processions, music, and local cuisine. These events provide a glimpse into the island's community spirit and deep-rooted traditions.

Dining and Local Cuisine

1. Traditional Eolian Dishes

- **Local Flavors**: Salina's cuisine is a celebration of Mediterranean flavors, with fresh seafood, locally grown vegetables, and the island's famous capers. Dishes like spaghetti alla Malvasia, stuffed squid, and granita are must-tries.

- **Where to Eat**: Popular dining spots include **Ristorante Da Alfredo** in Lingua, known for its granita and pane cunzato, and **Signum**, a Michelin-starred restaurant in Malfa offering gourmet Aeolian cuisine.

2. Local Delicacies

- **Capers**: Salina is renowned for its capers, which are a staple ingredient in Aeolian cooking. You can purchase jars of capers at local markets to take home a taste of the island.
- **Pastries and Sweets**: Try local sweets such as cannoli, made with fresh ricotta cheese, or cassata, a traditional Sicilian cake. These treats are often flavored with citrus and almonds, reflecting the island's agricultural bounty.

Practical Information

Best Time to Visit

- **Spring and Autumn**: These seasons offer mild weather and fewer tourists, making it the perfect time to enjoy outdoor activities and explore the island at a leisurely pace.
- **Summer**: If you enjoy warm weather and vibrant island life, summer is the busiest time on Salina, with festivals, beach activities, and bustling towns.

Accommodation

- **Where to Stay**: Salina offers a range of accommodation options, from luxury hotels like **Hotel Signum** in Malfa to charming bed and breakfasts. Whether you're looking for a beachfront stay or a peaceful retreat in the hills, Salina has something to suit every preference.

- **Booking Tips**: It's advisable to book accommodations well in advance, especially during the peak summer season, to secure the best options.

Salina, with its lush landscapes, rich cultural heritage, and serene atmosphere, offers a unique experience that captures the essence of the Aeolian Islands. Salina promises an unforgettable journey to one of Italy's most enchanting islands.

Stromboli

Stromboli, one of the most active volcanoes in the world and the northernmost of the Aeolian Islands, offers a unique blend of natural wonder and adventure. Known as the "Lighthouse of the Mediterranean," this island is a magnet for travelers seeking the excitement of witnessing volcanic activity and experiencing night hikes to the summit. Here's what you need to know for an unforgettable journey to Stromboli.

Getting to Stromboli

By Ferry

- **From Lipari**: Regular ferry services connect Lipari with Stromboli, with travel times varying depending on the type of ferry. The journey typically takes about 1.5 to 2 hours, offering stunning views of the archipelago along the way.
- **From Mainland Sicily**: Ferries from Milazzo and other Sicilian ports also serve Stromboli, making it accessible for day trips or longer stays.

By Hydrofoil

- **Faster Travel**: Hydrofoils provide a quicker alternative to ferries, reducing travel time and offering a smoother ride. Hydrofoils operate frequently during the summer months, catering to the high tourist demand.

By Private Boat

- **Tailored Experiences**: For a more personalized approach, consider hiring a private boat. This option allows you to explore the island at your own pace, with the flexibility to visit surrounding areas and hidden spots that are often inaccessible by larger vessels.

The Stromboli Volcano Experience

1. Understanding Stromboli's Volcanic Activity

- **Persistent Eruptions**: Stromboli is one of the few volcanoes in the world with continuous eruptions, which have been occurring for over 2,000 years. These regular explosions, known as "Strombolian eruptions," eject lava bombs, ash, and volcanic gases into the air, creating a spectacular natural display.
- **Sciara del Fuoco**: The Sciara del Fuoco (Stream of Fire) is a steep slope where most of the volcanic material flows into the sea. This area is the best vantage point to observe the eruptions safely, either from the sea or during a hike.

2. Guided Night Hikes to the Summit

- **Adventure and Safety**: The most exhilarating way to experience Stromboli is by embarking on a guided night hike to the summit. These hikes are led by experienced guides who ensure safety while providing insights into the volcano's behavior and history.

- **Starting the Hike**: Hikes typically start in the late afternoon from the village of San Vincenzo. The trail ascends gradually, offering panoramic views of the island and surrounding sea. The hike to the summit (924 meters above sea level) takes approximately 3 hours.
- **The Summit Experience**: Reaching the summit at dusk allows you to witness the glowing lava and eruptions against the night sky. The contrast between the dark sky and the fiery explosions creates an unforgettable spectacle.
- **What to Bring**: Sturdy hiking boots, a headlamp, warm clothing, and plenty of water are essential. A good level of fitness is required, as the hike is challenging and involves steep, uneven terrain.

3. Boat Tours for Volcano Watching

- **Up-Close Views from the Sea**: For those who prefer not to hike, boat tours offer an excellent alternative for viewing the volcano's activity. Boats anchor near the Sciara del Fuoco in the evening, providing a front-row seat to the eruptions.
- **Nighttime Excursions**: Night tours are particularly popular, as the darkness amplifies the visibility of the lava flows and explosions. Some tours include dinner on board, allowing you to enjoy the natural show in comfort.

Exploring Stromboli Beyond the Volcano

1. The Village of Stromboli

- **Charming Settlements**: The main village of Stromboli, also named Stromboli, is a picturesque settlement with whitewashed houses, narrow streets, and vibrant bougainvillea. The village exudes a tranquil charm, with small cafes, restaurants, and shops catering to visitors.
- **San Vincenzo Church**: Visit the Church of San Vincenzo, located in the heart of the village. This simple yet beautiful church offers a glimpse into the island's religious and cultural life.

2. Strombolicchio

- **A Geological Wonder**: Strombolicchio is a small volcanic rock located about 1.5 kilometers northeast of Stromboli. It is the remains of an ancient volcanic vent and stands as a dramatic monolith rising from the sea.
- **Boat Excursions**: Excursions to Strombolicchio are popular among visitors, offering opportunities for snorkeling in its crystal-clear waters and climbing the steep steps to the lighthouse at its summit.

3. Ginostra

- **Remote Village**: On the southwestern side of the island lies Ginostra, one of the most isolated villages in Italy. Accessible only by boat, Ginostra is a haven of peace and tranquility, with fewer than 40 permanent residents.
- **Porto di Pertuso**: The tiny harbor, Porto di Pertuso, is one of the smallest in the world. Visiting Ginostra offers a

glimpse into a way of life that has remained largely unchanged for centuries.

Experiencing the Natural Beauty of Stromboli

1. Black Sand Beaches

- **Unique Coastal Features**: Stromboli's volcanic nature is reflected in its beaches, which are characterized by fine black sand. Spiaggia di Ficogrande is the most popular beach, located near the main village, offering a beautiful contrast between the dark sand and the azure sea.
- **Swimming and Relaxation**: The beaches are ideal for swimming, sunbathing, and enjoying the serene island atmosphere. The warm waters are inviting, and the views of the volcano in the background add a unique touch to the experience.

2. Nature Walks

- **Exploring the Island's Flora**: In addition to the night hikes, Stromboli offers various nature walks that showcase its unique flora and landscapes. Trails around the island lead through lush vegetation, wildflowers, and ancient lava fields, providing a peaceful way to explore Stromboli's natural beauty.

3. Snorkeling and Diving

- **Marine Life Exploration**: The waters around Stromboli are rich in marine life, making it a fantastic destination for snorkeling and diving. Explore underwater caves, coral

reefs, and a variety of fish species in the clear, warm waters.
- **Diving Centers**: Several diving centers on the island offer guided dives and equipment rental. Whether you're a beginner or an experienced diver, Stromboli's underwater world offers something for everyone.

Local Culture and Cuisine

1. Stromboli's Culinary Scene

- **Traditional Dishes**: The island's cuisine is deeply rooted in its volcanic environment and maritime culture. Fresh seafood, locally grown vegetables, and unique dishes like pasta with swordfish or the famous Aeolian caponata are must-tries.
- **Where to Eat**: Popular dining spots include **Ristorante Punta Lena**, offering stunning sea views, and **La Lampara**, known for its fresh, locally sourced ingredients.

2. Local Festivals

- **Religious Celebrations**: Stromboli's cultural calendar includes several religious festivals, such as the Feast of San Bartolo, the island's patron saint. These events feature processions, music, and local food, offering visitors a chance to experience the island's traditions.
- **Volcano Festival**: Held annually in August, the Volcano Festival celebrates the island's unique relationship with its volcano. The festival includes music, dance, and cultural performances, all set against the backdrop of the active volcano.

Panarea

Panarea, the smallest of the Aeolian Islands, is renowned for its exclusive atmosphere, stunning scenery, and vibrant nightlife. Often described as a playground for the rich and famous, this island offers a blend of luxury, elegance, and natural beauty. Whether you're seeking a chic beach escape, high-end dining experiences, or a glimpse of celebrity life, Panarea promises an unforgettable experience of indulgence and style.

Getting to Panarea

By Ferry

- **From Lipari**: Regular ferry services connect Lipari with Panarea, with the journey taking around 45 minutes to an hour. The ferry ride offers picturesque views of the Aeolian archipelago.
- **From Mainland Sicily**: Panarea is also accessible by ferry from ports like Milazzo, with travel times varying depending on the type of ferry. High-speed hydrofoils are available for a faster journey.

By Private Yacht

- **Exclusive Arrival**: Many visitors arrive by private yacht, a popular choice for those seeking a more luxurious and personalized experience. The island's marina caters to yachts, offering mooring services and amenities for high-end travelers.

By Helicopter

- **Ultimate Luxury**: For the ultimate in luxury and convenience, helicopter transfers from Sicily or other parts of Italy are available. This option provides breathtaking aerial views of the islands and ensures a swift and stylish arrival.

The Luxury Experience in Panarea

1. Exclusive Accommodations

- **Luxury Hotels and Villas**: Panarea is home to some of the most luxurious hotels and private villas in the Aeolian Islands. These accommodations offer stunning sea views, infinity pools, and top-notch services that cater to the most discerning guests.
  - **Hotel Raya**: One of the island's most iconic hotels, known for its elegant design, panoramic views, and famous terrace bar where celebrities often gather.
  - **Capofaro Locanda & Malvasia**: A luxurious resort that combines traditional Aeolian architecture with modern amenities, offering a tranquil and exclusive retreat.
- **Private Villas**: Renting a private villa is a popular option for those seeking privacy and exclusivity. These villas often come with private pools, direct beach access, and personalized services such as private chefs and concierge.

2. High-End Dining and Nightlife

- **Gourmet Restaurants**: Panarea boasts a selection of gourmet restaurants that offer exquisite dining experiences.

Fresh seafood, local ingredients, and innovative culinary techniques are the highlights of the island's cuisine.
  - **Da Pina**: A renowned restaurant that offers fine dining with a focus on traditional Aeolian and Mediterranean dishes, complemented by an extensive wine list.
  - **Hycesia**: Known for its creative cuisine and beautiful garden setting, Hycesia offers a romantic dining experience with a touch of elegance.
- **Chic Bars and Clubs**: The nightlife in Panarea is sophisticated and lively, with chic bars and clubs that attract a glamorous crowd. The island's nightlife scene is famous for its late-night parties and fashionable venues.
  - **Hotel Raya Bar**: A must-visit for its stunning terrace with views of Stromboli's eruptions, offering a perfect spot for cocktails at sunset.
  - **Banacalii Club**: A trendy nightclub that hosts international DJs and attracts a stylish crowd looking to dance the night away.

3. Shopping for Luxury Goods

- **Designer Boutiques**: Panarea offers a selection of high-end boutiques that cater to fashion-conscious visitors. These shops offer everything from designer clothing and accessories to unique jewelry and handcrafted items.
  - **Boutique Erica**: A favorite among fashion lovers, offering a curated selection of Italian and international designer brands.
  - **Lo Scrigno di Ale**: A luxury boutique known for its elegant clothing, jewelry, and exclusive beachwear,

perfect for those looking to shop for high-quality pieces.
- **Local Artisan Shops**: In addition to luxury goods, Panarea also features shops that sell locally made crafts and souvenirs. These include hand-painted ceramics, artisanal jewelry, and other unique items that reflect the island's heritage.

Exploring Panarea's Natural Beauty

1. Stunning Beaches

- **Cala Junco**: One of Panarea's most famous beaches, Cala Junco is a picturesque cove surrounded by rocky cliffs and crystal-clear waters. The beach is accessible via a short hike and is perfect for swimming, snorkeling, and sunbathing.
- **Zimmari Beach**: Another popular beach on the island, Zimmari Beach is known for its beautiful red sand and tranquil atmosphere. The beach is ideal for a relaxing day by the sea, with shallow waters that are perfect for swimming.
- **Private Beach Access**: Many luxury villas and hotels offer private beach access, providing guests with exclusive and secluded spots to enjoy the island's natural beauty.

2. Scenic Walks and Hiking

- **Hiking to Cala Junco**: The hike to Cala Junco is one of the most popular on the island, offering stunning views of the coastline and the surrounding sea. The trail is relatively easy and can be enjoyed by visitors of all fitness levels.

- **Exploring the Island's Landscapes**: For those looking to explore more of Panarea's natural beauty, the island offers several scenic walks that take you through its unique landscapes. Trails lead through fragrant Mediterranean vegetation, past ancient ruins, and up to viewpoints that offer breathtaking panoramas of the surrounding islands.

3. **Boat Excursions and Island Hopping**

- **Luxury Yacht Tours**: One of the best ways to experience Panarea is by sea. Luxury yacht tours offer personalized excursions around the island, visiting hidden coves, sea caves, and nearby islets. These tours often include gourmet meals, snorkeling stops, and the chance to explore uninhabited islands.
- **Visiting the Islets**: Panarea is surrounded by several smaller islets, such as Basiluzzo and Lisca Bianca, which are perfect for day trips. These islets offer pristine waters for swimming and snorkeling, as well as opportunities to explore volcanic formations and ancient ruins.

4. **Diving and Snorkeling**

- **World-Class Diving Sites**: Panarea is a popular destination for diving enthusiasts, with several world-class diving sites nearby. The clear waters around the island offer excellent visibility, allowing divers to explore underwater caves, coral reefs, and marine life.
- **Snorkeling Spots**: For those who prefer snorkeling, Panarea's beaches and coves offer plenty of opportunities to explore the underwater world. The waters around the

islets are particularly rich in marine life, making them ideal for snorkeling adventures.

Cultural and Historical Highlights

1. The Prehistoric Village of Capo Milazzese

- **Ancient Ruins**: Located on the southern tip of the island, the prehistoric village of Capo Milazzese is an important archaeological site that dates back to the Bronze Age. The site features the remains of ancient huts and offers insights into the early inhabitants of Panarea.
- **Panoramic Views**: The site is perched on a cliff overlooking the sea, offering stunning views of the surrounding islands and the crystal-clear waters below. The hike to the site is relatively easy and provides a fascinating glimpse into the island's ancient past.

2. San Pietro Village

- **Charming Streets**: San Pietro is the main village on Panarea, known for its charming streets, whitewashed houses, and vibrant bougainvillea. The village is the center of the island's social life, with numerous cafes, restaurants, and shops.
- **Cultural Landmarks**: While exploring San Pietro, visitors can discover several cultural landmarks, including the Church of San Pietro, a beautiful example of Aeolian architecture, and the small local museum that showcases artifacts from the island's history.

3. Festivals and Events

- **The Feast of San Pietro**: The Feast of San Pietro, held on June 29th, is the island's most important religious and cultural event. The celebration includes a procession,

fireworks, and traditional music, offering visitors a chance to experience Panarea's local traditions.
- **Summer Concerts and Events**: During the summer months, Panarea hosts a variety of cultural events, including open-air concerts, art exhibitions, and fashion shows. These events add to the island's glamorous atmosphere and provide entertainment for visitors.

Practical Information for Visiting Panarea

1. Best Time to Visit

- **Summer Luxury**: Panarea is at its most vibrant during the summer months, from June to September, when the island comes alive with tourists, luxury yachts, and high-end events. The warm weather and clear skies make it the perfect time to enjoy the beaches and nightlife.
- **Spring and Autumn Tranquility**: For those seeking a quieter experience, spring (April to May) and autumn (October) offer milder weather and fewer crowds. During these seasons, the island retains its charm and beauty while offering a more relaxed atmosphere.

2. Health and Safety

- **Sun Protection**: The sun can be intense on Panarea, especially during the summer. Visitors should take precautions by wearing sunscreen, hats, and light clothing to avoid sunburn and dehydration.

3. Environmental Considerations

- **Sustainability Initiatives**: Panarea is committed to preserving its natural beauty and environment. Visitors are encouraged to respect the island's ecosystems by avoiding littering, minimizing plastic use, and staying on marked paths during hikes.
- **Energy Conservation**: As part of its sustainability efforts, Panarea promotes energy conservation, with many hotels and villas using solar power and other eco-friendly technologies.

Panarea, with its blend of luxury, natural beauty, and vibrant culture, offers an unparalleled experience in the Aeolian Islands.

NIGHTLIFE AND ENTERTAINMENT IN LIPARI

As the sun sets on Lipari, the island transforms into a lively hub of nightlife and entertainment, offering something for every type of traveler. The evenings here can be as relaxed or as vibrant as you wish, with options ranging from cozy wine bars to bustling nightclubs.

Bars and Nightclubs in Lipari

Lipari offers a vibrant nightlife scene with a variety of bars and nightclubs to suit every mood and preference. Whether you're looking for a casual evening with friends, a romantic night out, or a lively dance party, the island's establishments cater to all.

Popular Bars

1. **Sea-View Bars**
   - **Tropical Bar**: Located along the picturesque harbor, Tropical Bar is a favorite among locals and tourists alike. The bar's outdoor terrace offers stunning views of the marina and the neighboring islands, making it an ideal spot for a sunset cocktail. The relaxed atmosphere, combined with an extensive drink menu featuring local wines, signature cocktails, and refreshing spritzers, makes it perfect for unwinding after a day of exploration.
   - **Chitarra Bar**: Nestled in the heart of Lipari's old town, Chitarra Bar is known for its bohemian vibe and artistic ambiance. This cozy spot is popular for

its eclectic music playlist, which ranges from jazz to indie, and its creative cocktail offerings. The bar also hosts occasional open-mic nights, adding to its lively and welcoming atmosphere.

2. **Wine Bars**
    - **E Pulera**: A charming wine bar that specializes in showcasing the best of Aeolian wines, E Pulera is perfect for those looking to sample the island's rich viticultural heritage. The bar offers a curated selection of local wines, including the famous Malvasia delle Lipari, paired with delicious antipasti. The intimate setting, with its traditional Aeolian decor and candle-lit tables, makes it a popular choice for a romantic evening.
    - **Enoteca d'Ambra**: Situated in the bustling Piazza Mazzini, Enoteca d'Ambra is a trendy wine bar that attracts a sophisticated crowd. The bar offers an extensive list of wines from across Italy, with a particular focus on Sicilian and Aeolian varieties. The knowledgeable staff are happy to guide you through their selection, making it an excellent choice for wine enthusiasts.

3. **Cocktail Lounges**
    - **La Piazzetta**: Located in the center of Lipari, La Piazzetta is known for its chic and modern ambiance. The lounge offers a wide range of cocktails, from classic recipes to innovative creations, all made with high-quality ingredients. The sleek interior, comfortable seating, and lively yet relaxed atmosphere make it a great place to start your night out.

- **Porto Vecchio Lounge**: Overlooking the old port, Porto Vecchio Lounge combines elegant decor with a lively atmosphere. The bar is known for its expertly crafted cocktails and live DJ sets, which keep the energy high throughout the evening. It's a popular spot for both locals and visitors, offering a stylish setting to enjoy Lipari's nightlife.

Nightclubs

1. **White Beach Club**
    - **Overview**: White Beach Club is one of Lipari's premier nightclubs, famous for its beachfront location and vibrant parties. The club features an outdoor dance floor that opens directly onto the beach, allowing guests to dance under the stars to the sounds of international DJs. With a mix of electronic, dance, and pop music, White Beach Club attracts a diverse crowd looking for a high-energy night out.
    - **Special Events**: The club regularly hosts themed parties, live performances, and guest DJ appearances, making it a hotspot for nightlife in Lipari. Whether you're celebrating a special occasion or simply looking to dance the night away, White Beach Club offers an unforgettable experience.
2. **Turmalin**
    - **Overview**: Turmalin is a stylish and upscale nightclub located in the heart of Lipari. Known for its exclusive vibe and elegant decor, the club attracts a fashionable crowd. The interior features

modern design elements with ambient lighting, plush seating, and a state-of-the-art sound system.
- **Music and Atmosphere**: Turmalin offers a mix of house, techno, and R&B music, with live DJ sets that keep the dance floor buzzing. The club also features a VIP section for those looking to enjoy a more private and luxurious experience. With its sophisticated atmosphere and top-notch service, Turmalin is a must-visit for nightlife enthusiasts.

Live Music Venues and Shows in Lipari

Lipari's live music scene is an integral part of its cultural landscape, offering a range of venues and performances that cater to different tastes. From traditional Italian folk music to contemporary genres, the island's live music venues provide entertainment that enhances the Lipari experience.

Popular Live Music Venues

1. **Bar La Precchia**
    - **Overview**: Located in a historic building near the main square, Bar La Precchia is a beloved live music venue that showcases a variety of genres. The bar has a rustic charm, with wooden beams, stone walls, and a cozy atmosphere that makes it a favorite among locals and visitors.
    - **Music and Performances**: Bar La Precchia hosts regular live performances, featuring local bands, solo artists, and occasionally, international acts. The music ranges from traditional Sicilian folk songs to jazz and blues, providing an eclectic mix that appeals to all audiences. The intimate setting allows

for close interaction with the performers, creating a unique and engaging experience.

2. **Chiesa di San Bartolomeo**
   - **Overview**: The Church of San Bartolomeo, the patron saint of Lipari, is not only a place of worship but also a venue for cultural events, including live music concerts. The church's stunning architecture and acoustics make it an exceptional setting for classical music performances.
   - **Special Concerts**: Throughout the year, the church hosts a variety of concerts, including choral performances, classical music recitals, and special events during religious festivals. These concerts often feature talented musicians from the Aeolian Islands and beyond, offering a spiritual and cultural experience that resonates with the island's rich history.

3. **Ristorante Filippino**
   - **Overview**: Ristorante Filippino, one of Lipari's oldest and most renowned restaurants, also doubles as a live music venue in the evenings. Known for its traditional Aeolian cuisine, the restaurant offers a unique dining experience with live music performances that enhance the ambiance.
   - **Music and Dining Experience**: Guests can enjoy a delicious meal while listening to live performances of Italian ballads, classical guitar, and more. The combination of fine dining and live music creates a memorable evening, where the sounds of the musicians complement the flavors of the local dishes.

Music Festivals and Events

1. **Lipari Music Festival**
   - **Overview**: The Lipari Music Festival is a highlight of the island's cultural calendar, attracting musicians and music lovers from around the world. Held annually during the summer, the festival features a series of concerts, workshops, and masterclasses across various genres, including classical, jazz, and world music.
   - **Venues and Performances**: The festival takes place in some of Lipari's most iconic locations, including the ancient amphitheater, historic churches, and outdoor piazzas. The diverse lineup of performances offers something for every music enthusiast, making it a must-attend event for visitors during the festival season.
2. **Jazz on the Rocks**
   - **Overview**: Jazz on the Rocks is an annual jazz festival held on the cliffs of Lipari, offering a breathtaking backdrop of the Tyrrhenian Sea. The festival celebrates jazz music in all its forms, from traditional to contemporary, and features performances by both established and emerging artists.
   - **Atmosphere and Experience**: The unique setting of the festival creates an intimate and immersive experience, where the music blends seamlessly with the natural beauty of the island. The event often includes jam sessions, workshops, and late-night performances, making it a dynamic and exciting part of Lipari's cultural scene.

Lipari's bars, nightclubs, and live music venues offer a diverse and vibrant nightlife experience that caters to all tastes. Whether you're looking to dance the night away at a trendy nightclub, enjoy a glass of wine while listening to live music, or immerse yourself in the island's rich cultural traditions, Lipari has something to offer every visitor.

Evening Activities in Lipari

As the day winds down in Lipari, the island offers a range of evening activities that allow visitors to experience its beauty in a new light. From the glow of the setting sun reflecting on the sea to the twinkling stars in the clear night sky, Lipari's evenings are filled with opportunities for relaxation and exploration.

Sunset Cruises

One of the most enchanting ways to end your day in Lipari is by taking a sunset cruise around the island. These cruises provide a unique perspective of Lipari and its surrounding waters, as the setting sun casts a warm, golden hue over the landscape.

- **Experience**: Aboard a comfortable boat, you'll sail along the island's rugged coastline, passing by secluded coves, cliffs, and volcanic rock formations. As the sun dips below the horizon, the sky transforms into a palette of vibrant colors, creating a mesmerizing backdrop for your evening.
- **Amenities**: Many sunset cruises include complimentary drinks and snacks, allowing you to toast the end of the day with a glass of local wine or a refreshing cocktail. Some cruises even offer live music on board, adding to the romantic atmosphere.
- **Special Cruises**: For a more personalized experience, consider booking a private sunset cruise. These exclusive

trips can be tailored to your preferences, whether you want a quiet evening for two or a lively gathering with friends.

Stargazing

Lipari's clear, unpolluted skies make it an ideal location for stargazing. As night falls, the stars emerge in their full glory, providing a breathtaking view of the cosmos.

- **Best Spots**: The island offers several great stargazing locations, from quiet beaches to hilltops with panoramic views. For the best experience, head to the less populated areas of the island, where the absence of city lights allows the stars to shine even brighter.
- **Guided Stargazing Tours**: To enhance your stargazing experience, consider joining a guided stargazing tour. These tours are led by knowledgeable guides who will help you identify constellations, planets, and other celestial objects. Some tours also provide telescopes for a closer look at the night sky.
- **Astronomy Events**: Throughout the year, Lipari hosts various astronomy events, including night sky photography workshops and special viewing sessions during meteor showers. These events offer a unique opportunity to learn more about the stars and deepen your appreciation for the night sky.

Nighttime Walks

For those who enjoy a leisurely stroll, Lipari's charming streets and coastal paths take on a magical quality in the evening. The island's cool evening breeze, combined with the soft glow of streetlights, creates a peaceful and romantic atmosphere.

- **Old Town Walks**: Exploring Lipari's old town at night is a delightful experience. The narrow cobblestone streets, historic buildings, and lively piazzas are beautifully lit, offering a different perspective of the town. Along the way, you'll pass by quaint cafes, artisan shops, and churches, many of which stay open late into the evening.
- **Coastal Walks**: For a more scenic walk, head to one of Lipari's coastal paths. The paths along the western coast, near the Quattrocchi Viewpoint, are particularly popular for evening walks. As you stroll, you'll enjoy stunning views of the sea and the distant lights of the neighboring islands.

Evening Markets and Street Fairs

Lipari's evening markets and street fairs are vibrant events that bring the local culture to life. These markets are held during the summer months and offer a wide range of goods, from handmade crafts to local delicacies.

- **What to Expect**: At these markets, you'll find stalls selling everything from artisanal jewelry and ceramics to fresh produce and traditional Aeolian treats. The lively atmosphere is enhanced by street performers, live music, and the warm, welcoming spirit of the locals.
- **Best Locations**: The main market is usually held in Piazza Mazzini or along the waterfront promenade. These locations are perfect for an evening of shopping, dining, and soaking in the local culture.

Outdoor Cinemas

During the summer, Lipari offers outdoor cinema experiences, where visitors can watch movies under the stars. These screenings are often held in scenic locations, such as parks or seaside venues, creating a unique and enjoyable way to spend an evening.

- **Film Selection**: The films shown range from classic Italian cinema to contemporary international releases. Whether you're a film buff or just looking for a relaxing evening, the outdoor cinema offers a laid-back, entertaining option.
- **What to Bring**: Bring a blanket or a comfortable chair, and settle in for a cozy evening. Some venues also offer refreshments, including popcorn, drinks, and local snacks.

Dining Al Fresco

Evening dining in Lipari is a delightful experience, with many restaurants offering al fresco seating that allows you to enjoy the island's pleasant evening temperatures.

- **Seafood Dinners**: Lipari's restaurants are renowned for their seafood, and there's no better way to enjoy it than with a view of the sea. Many eateries along the waterfront offer fresh, locally caught fish and seafood, prepared in traditional Aeolian styles. The combination of delicious food, fine wine, and the gentle sea breeze creates a perfect evening setting.
- **Piazza Dining**: For a more lively atmosphere, consider dining in one of Lipari's piazzas. The open-air restaurants here offer a variety of dishes, from pizza and pasta to more elaborate regional specialties. As you dine, you'll be surrounded by the buzz of evening activity, with street performers, locals, and tourists alike enjoying the night.

EXPLORING FAMILY-FRIENDLY LIPARI

Lipari is a fantastic destination for families seeking a mix of adventure, relaxation, and cultural experiences. With its beautiful beaches, fascinating history, and variety of outdoor activities, the island offers something for every member of the family to enjoy.

Beaches and Swimming

Lipari is home to numerous family-friendly beaches where children and adults alike can enjoy the crystal-clear waters of the Tyrrhenian Sea.

- **Spiaggia di Canneto**: This popular beach features soft sand and shallow waters, making it an ideal spot for young children to play and swim safely. The beach is well-equipped with facilities such as sun loungers, umbrellas, and nearby cafes, ensuring a comfortable day by the sea for the whole family.
- **Spiaggia Bianca**: Known for its stunning white pebbles and turquoise waters, Spiaggia Bianca offers a more secluded beach experience. It's a great place for families to enjoy a peaceful day, with plenty of opportunities for snorkeling and exploring the underwater world.

Outdoor Adventures

For families who love to explore nature, Lipari offers a variety of outdoor activities that are both fun and educational.

- **Hiking**: The island's hiking trails are suitable for all ages, with paths that range from easy walks to more challenging treks. The Quattrocchi Viewpoint hike, for example, is a family-friendly route that rewards hikers with breathtaking views of the surrounding islands and the sea.
- **Boat Tours**: A boat tour around Lipari is a must-do for families. These tours often include stops at nearby islands, opportunities for swimming and snorkeling, and the chance to see the island's dramatic coastline from the water. Some boat tours are specifically designed for families, with guides who provide interesting facts about the area's geology and marine life.

Historical and Cultural Experiences

Lipari's rich history and culture provide plenty of opportunities for educational and entertaining family outings.

- **Museo Archeologico Regionale Eoliano**: This archaeological museum is a fascinating place for families to learn about the history of the Aeolian Islands. The museum's exhibits include ancient artifacts, pottery, and interactive displays that bring the past to life for younger visitors.
- **Lipari Castle**: Exploring the ancient Lipari Castle is like stepping back in time. The castle's ramparts offer stunning views of the island, and the surrounding archaeological park is a great place for children to roam and discover remnants of Lipari's ancient civilizations.

Family-Friendly Dining

When it comes to dining, Lipari offers numerous restaurants that cater to families, with menus featuring local dishes as well as kid-friendly options.

- **Pizzerias**: Italian cuisine is always a hit with children, and Lipari's pizzerias serve up delicious, wood-fired pizzas that the whole family will love. Many restaurants also offer outdoor seating, allowing families to enjoy their meal while taking in the island's beautiful scenery.
- **Gelato Shops**: No family trip to Italy would be complete without indulging in some gelato. Lipari's gelato shops offer a wide variety of flavors, from classic chocolate and vanilla to more adventurous options like pistachio and lemon.

Playgrounds and Parks

For families traveling with younger children, Lipari has several parks and playgrounds where kids can burn off energy while parents relax.

- **Piazza Mazzini**: This central square in Lipari town is a popular gathering spot for locals and visitors alike. It's a great place for children to play while parents enjoy a coffee at one of the nearby cafes.
- **Public Parks**: Lipari's public parks provide green spaces where families can enjoy a picnic or a leisurely walk. The parks are well-maintained and offer a peaceful retreat from the bustling town center.

Events and Festivals

Throughout the year, Lipari hosts a variety of festivals and events that are perfect for families.

- **San Bartolomeo Festival**: Held in August, this festival celebrates Lipari's patron saint with parades, fireworks, and live music. The festival's lively atmosphere and colorful displays make it a memorable experience for visitors of all ages.
- **Food Festivals**: Lipari's food festivals are a great way for families to sample local delicacies and learn about the island's culinary traditions. These events often include cooking demonstrations, tastings, and activities for children.

Lipari is an ideal destination for families, offering a blend of natural beauty, cultural richness, and outdoor fun. With its welcoming atmosphere and wide range of activities, Lipari ensures that every family member has a memorable and enjoyable vacation.

Kid-Friendly Attractions and Activities in Lipari

Lipari is a fantastic destination for families with children, offering a variety of attractions and activities that cater specifically to younger visitors. From exploring ancient castles to enjoying interactive museum exhibits and outdoor adventures, there's plenty to keep kids entertained and engaged.

Museo Archeologico Regionale Eoliano

A visit to the Museo Archeologico Regionale Eoliano is both educational and fun for children. This museum houses an impressive collection of artifacts from the Aeolian Islands, dating back thousands of years.

- **Interactive Exhibits**: The museum features several interactive displays that make learning about history more engaging for children. They can see ancient pottery, tools, and even shipwrecks, all of which provide a glimpse into the lives of the island's early inhabitants.
- **Family-Friendly Workshops**: The museum often hosts workshops and activities designed for children, where they can participate in hands-on experiences like pottery making or learning about archaeology through guided activities.

Lipari Castle

Lipari Castle, perched on a hill overlooking the town, is a great place for kids to explore and let their imaginations run wild.

- **Exploring the Fortress**: The castle's ancient walls, towers, and walkways offer plenty of nooks and crannies for children to explore. The historical setting allows kids to feel like they've stepped into a medieval adventure.
- **Archaeological Park**: Surrounding the castle, the archaeological park features ruins and ancient structures that kids can wander through. It's a wonderful place for a family picnic, with plenty of open space for children to play.

Beaches and Water Activities

Lipari's beaches are perfect for family days out, offering safe, shallow waters and plenty of activities for kids.

- **Spiaggia di Canneto**: This beach is ideal for families, with calm waters where kids can swim and play safely. The beach is well-equipped with amenities, including snack bars and ice cream stands, making it easy to spend a full day here.
- **Snorkeling and Swimming**: Older children will enjoy snorkeling in the clear waters around Lipari. Several beaches offer equipment rentals and lessons, making it easy for kids to discover the underwater world and its vibrant marine life.

Boat Tours

A boat tour around Lipari is an exciting adventure for kids, offering them a chance to see the island from a new perspective.

- **Island Hopping**: Many boat tours include stops at nearby islands, where families can explore different beaches, swim in hidden coves, and even visit other volcanic islands. The thrill of being on the water and the possibility of spotting dolphins or other marine animals make these tours a hit with children.
- **Glass-Bottom Boats**: For a closer look at the underwater world without getting wet, consider a glass-bottom boat tour. These tours allow kids to see fish, coral, and other sea creatures up close, all from the safety of the boat.

Hiking and Nature Walks

Lipari's natural beauty can be enjoyed by families through its various hiking trails and nature walks, many of which are suitable for children.

- **Easy Trails**: There are several easy hiking trails around Lipari that offer stunning views without being too strenuous for young children. The Quattrocchi Viewpoint is one such trail, providing breathtaking panoramas of the coastline and nearby islands.
- **Nature Walks**: Guided nature walks are a great way for kids to learn about the local flora and fauna. These walks often include educational elements, such as identifying different plants or learning about the island's volcanic origins.

Playgrounds and Public Parks

For families with young children, Lipari's playgrounds and parks offer a safe and fun environment for play and relaxation.

- **Piazza Mazzini**: This central square is a popular spot for families, with a small playground where children can climb, slide, and swing. The surrounding cafes and gelato shops make it easy for parents to relax while the kids play.
- **Public Gardens**: Lipari's public gardens are peaceful spots where families can enjoy a picnic or simply relax. These green spaces often have shaded areas, making them perfect for a break from the sun.

Local Events and Festivals

Lipari's festivals and local events are family-friendly and offer a fun way to immerse children in the island's culture.

- **San Bartolomeo Festival**: This annual event, held in honor of Lipari's patron saint, features parades, fireworks, and live music. The festive atmosphere is exciting for children, who can enjoy the colorful displays and traditional performances.
- **Summer Festivals**: During the summer, Lipari hosts a variety of cultural events, including open-air concerts, food festivals, and street performances. These events are often geared toward families, with activities and entertainment for children.

Educational Tours

For curious kids, Lipari offers educational tours that combine learning with adventure.

- **Volcano Tours**: Guided tours that focus on the island's volcanic history are both educational and exciting. Kids can learn about the science behind volcanoes and even visit active volcanic sites on nearby islands like Stromboli.
- **Marine Biology Tours**: Some boat tours and coastal walks include a focus on marine biology, where guides teach children about the local sea life, ecosystems, and the importance of conservation.

Overall, Lipari's blend of natural beauty, historical sites, and family-oriented activities ensures that kids have plenty to do, see, and learn.

Family Accommodation Options in Lipari

Finding the right place to stay is key to ensuring a comfortable and enjoyable family vacation. Lipari offers a range of family-friendly accommodation options, from spacious hotels with child-friendly amenities to cozy apartments and budget-friendly alternatives. Here's a guide to the best family accommodations on the island, ensuring that every member of the family has a great time.

Family-Friendly Hotels

Several hotels on Lipari cater specifically to families, offering amenities like pools, playgrounds, and family-sized rooms.

- **Hotel Aktea**: Located near the Marina Lunga harbor, Hotel Aktea is a popular choice for families. The hotel offers spacious rooms that can accommodate families of various sizes, along with a large outdoor swimming pool and a garden area where children can play. The hotel's restaurant features a kid-friendly menu, making mealtime easy and enjoyable.
- **Hotel Villa Enrica**: Perched on a hill with stunning views of the sea, Hotel Villa Enrica is a boutique hotel that welcomes families. The hotel offers family rooms with extra beds or adjoining rooms, ensuring plenty of space for everyone. The outdoor pool and surrounding terraces provide a relaxing environment for both parents and children, and the hotel offers shuttle services to nearby beaches.

Apartments and Vacation Rentals

For families seeking more space and the convenience of self-catering, apartments and vacation rentals are an excellent option.

- **Case Vacanze Arcobaleno**: This collection of holiday apartments is perfect for families looking for a home-away-from-home experience. Each apartment comes with a fully equipped kitchen, allowing families to prepare their meals. The apartments are spacious, with separate bedrooms for parents and children, and many feature balconies or terraces with views of the sea.
- **Villa Sea Rose**: Located close to the center of Lipari town, Villa Sea Rose offers family-sized apartments within walking distance of restaurants, shops, and the beach. The apartments are well-furnished and equipped with kitchens, making it easy to accommodate the needs of a family. The property also has a garden area where children can play safely.

Resorts with Family Amenities

For families seeking a resort experience with all-inclusive amenities, Lipari offers a few options that cater specifically to families.

- **Hotel Tritone**: This luxurious resort offers a range of family-friendly services, including a children's pool, babysitting services, and family suites with extra beds. The resort's spa and wellness center provides a relaxing escape for parents, while the hotel's proximity to the beach ensures plenty of fun for the whole family. The on-site restaurant serves a variety of dishes, including options that appeal to younger palates.

- **Residence La Giara**: Located close to Lipari's town center, this residence offers apartment-style accommodations with the added benefits of a resort. Families can enjoy the outdoor pool, garden, and BBQ facilities, as well as easy access to nearby attractions. The residence provides spacious two-bedroom apartments, perfect for families, and a breakfast service to start the day off right.

Budget-Friendly Options

For families traveling on a budget, Lipari offers several affordable accommodation options without sacrificing comfort or convenience.

- **Hotel Oriente**: This budget-friendly hotel is centrally located, offering easy access to Lipari's main attractions. The rooms are clean and comfortable, with options for families that include extra beds or adjoining rooms. The hotel provides a continental breakfast, and the staff are known for being particularly helpful with families, offering advice on the best local activities for kids.
- **B&B Il Cappero**: A charming bed and breakfast, Il Cappero offers affordable rooms with a personal touch. The B&B's owner is known for being welcoming to families, providing recommendations for family-friendly activities and restaurants. Rooms are simple but comfortable, and the B&B's location makes it easy to explore Lipari on foot.

Camping and Outdoor Stays

For families who love the outdoors, camping and other alternative stays can be a fun and budget-friendly option.

- **Camping Baia Unci**: Located near Canneto Beach, Camping Baia Unci offers a unique stay experience in Lipari. Families can choose from traditional camping pitches or rent one of the on-site bungalows, which come equipped with basic kitchen facilities. The campsite features a playground for children, and the beach is just a short walk away, making it an ideal base for families who want to spend their days swimming and sunbathing.
- **Agriturismo La Dolce Vita**: For a more rural experience, this farm stay provides an opportunity for families to enjoy Lipari's countryside. The property offers family rooms and a variety of outdoor activities, including hiking, animal feeding, and cooking classes. The farm stay also provides homemade meals using local ingredients, ensuring a truly authentic experience.

Tips for Choosing Family Accommodation

When selecting family accommodation in Lipari, consider the following tips to ensure a comfortable stay:

- **Location**: Choose accommodation that is close to the attractions and activities your family plans to visit. Staying near the beach or town center can save time and make it easier to explore with children.
- **Facilities**: Look for accommodations that offer child-friendly facilities such as swimming pools, playgrounds, or family-sized rooms. Some hotels and resorts also offer

babysitting services or kids' clubs, giving parents a chance to relax.
- **Self-Catering**: For longer stays, consider apartments or vacation rentals with kitchen facilities. This allows you to prepare meals at your convenience and can be more budget-friendly.
- **Reviews**: Reading reviews from other families can provide valuable insights into the suitability of an accommodation. Look for comments on the comfort, cleanliness, and family-friendliness of the property.

Lipari's diverse range of family accommodation options ensures that every family can find the perfect place to stay, whether they're seeking luxury, budget options, or a unique outdoor experience. With the right choice, your family vacation on this beautiful island will be both comfortable and memorable.

Tips for Traveling with Children to Lipari

Traveling with children can be a rewarding experience, but it also requires careful planning to ensure a smooth and enjoyable trip. Lipari, with its family-friendly attractions and relaxed atmosphere, is an ideal destination for a family vacation. Here are some comprehensive tips to help you make the most of your visit to Lipari when traveling with children.

1. Plan Ahead and Book Early

- **Accommodation**: Family-friendly accommodations in Lipari can fill up quickly, especially during the peak travel season. Booking early ensures you get the best options, such as hotels with swimming pools, connecting rooms, or self-catering apartments that offer the convenience of preparing meals at your own pace.
- **Transportation**: If you plan to rent a car, reserve it well in advance. Ensure the car is equipped with child safety seats if needed. Similarly, book ferry tickets early, particularly if you're traveling with a larger family, as ferries to and from Lipari can get crowded during the summer months.

2. Pack Smart and Light

- **Essential Items**: When packing, include essential items like snacks, water bottles, and a first-aid kit with child-specific medications. Also, pack extra clothes for changes, as children tend to get messy or wet, especially at the beach.
- **Travel Gear**: If you have younger children, bring a lightweight stroller for easy navigation through Lipari's cobblestone streets and hilly areas. A baby carrier might

also be useful for hiking or visiting less accessible attractions.
- **Beach Gear**: Don't forget to pack beach essentials like sunscreen, hats, swimwear, and water shoes. Many beaches in Lipari have pebbly shores, so water shoes can help protect little feet.

3. Keep Kids Entertained During Travel

- **Travel Games and Activities**: Long journeys can be challenging for children, so bring travel games, coloring books, or tablets loaded with their favorite movies or educational apps to keep them occupied during ferry rides or flights.
- **Interactive Maps**: Engage older children by involving them in the trip planning process. Give them a map of Lipari and let them help choose which attractions to visit. This not only keeps them entertained but also sparks their interest in the destination.

4. Prioritize Safety

- **Childproofing**: If staying in an apartment or rental, check for safety features like stair gates, secure balconies, and locked cabinets. You may want to bring outlet covers and other childproofing items for added peace of mind.
- **Water Safety**: Always supervise children closely at the beach or pool. While many beaches in Lipari are safe for swimming, currents can be strong in some areas. Make sure young children wear life jackets if they're not strong swimmers.
- **Health Precautions**: Be mindful of sun exposure, and ensure children stay hydrated, especially when exploring

the island on hot days. Carry insect repellent, particularly if you plan to visit nature reserves or go hiking.

5. Plan Child-Friendly Activities

- **Mix of Activities**: Balance your itinerary with a mix of active and relaxing activities. While exploring historic sites and museums can be educational, kids will also appreciate time at the beach, in a playground, or enjoying an ice cream in the town square.
- **Breaks and Naps**: Plan for regular breaks and, if needed, nap times. This ensures that children don't become overtired or cranky, which can make sightseeing difficult. Consider visiting major attractions in the morning and allowing for a more relaxed afternoon.

6. Explore Family-Friendly Dining Options

- **Local Cuisine**: While Lipari offers a variety of dining options, it's a good idea to find restaurants that offer kid-friendly menus or are open to preparing simple meals for younger children. Italian cuisine is generally child-friendly, with pasta, pizza, and gelato being favorites among kids.
- **Eating Out**: Many restaurants in Lipari are family-friendly and welcome children. Look for places with outdoor seating where children can move around more freely. Some restaurants also provide high chairs and booster seats.

7. Embrace the Local Culture

- **Language Learning**: Teach your children a few basic Italian phrases before your trip. Simple greetings like "ciao" (hello) and "grazie" (thank you) can make them feel more connected to the local culture and more confident during interactions.

- **Cultural Respect**: Encourage children to respect local customs and traditions. For example, explain the importance of quietness in churches or during local festivals. Participating in cultural events, like the San Bartolomeo Festival, can be a fun and educational experience for kids.

8. Consider Travel Insurance

- **Comprehensive Coverage**: Ensure your travel insurance covers the whole family, including any potential medical emergencies or travel disruptions. This provides peace of mind, knowing that you're prepared for unexpected situations.
- **Specific Needs**: If any of your children have specific medical needs or allergies, make sure these are covered by your insurance, and carry relevant medical documentation or prescriptions.

9. Stay Flexible

- **Adaptability**: Traveling with children often requires flexibility. Be prepared to adjust your plans if a child becomes tired, unwell, or simply needs a break. Keeping a flexible itinerary allows you to make the most of your family vacation without feeling stressed.
- **Local Advice**: Don't hesitate to ask locals for advice on family-friendly spots or activities. Often, they can point you toward lesser-known beaches, quiet parks, or restaurants that are particularly welcoming to families.

10. Capture the Memories

- **Family Photos**: Take plenty of photos to capture the special moments of your family trip. Consider creating a travel journal with your children, where they can draw pictures, write about their favorite experiences, or collect small souvenirs like tickets or postcards.
- **Souvenirs**: Allow children to pick out a small souvenir from their trip. Whether it's a piece of local pottery, a postcard, or a shell from the beach, these items can serve as cherished reminders of your family's adventure in Lipari.

Lipari's relaxed pace, welcoming atmosphere, and range of activities make it an ideal destination for families. With a bit of preparation and these helpful tips, you can ensure that your trip to Lipari with children is a memorable and enjoyable experience for everyone involved.

WELLNESS AND RELAXATION IN LIPARI

Lipari is not just a destination for adventure and exploration but also a sanctuary for those seeking wellness and relaxation. The island's natural beauty, tranquil atmosphere, and soothing environment provide the perfect backdrop for unwinding and rejuvenating both body and mind.

Spas and Wellness Centers in Lipari

The island's spas and wellness centers are renowned for their serene settings, expert treatments, and the use of natural, local ingredients. Do you want to indulge in a luxurious spa day or embark on a comprehensive wellness retreat, Lipari offers a variety of options to cater to your needs.

Luxury Spas with Panoramic Views

Many of Lipari's top hotels and resorts house state-of-the-art spa facilities that offer a range of treatments designed to relax and rejuvenate. These luxury spas are often situated in locations that provide stunning views of the surrounding sea, hills, or volcanic landscapes, adding to the overall sense of tranquility.

- **Treatment Options**: Guests can choose from an extensive menu of treatments, including massages, facials, body scrubs, and wraps. Many of these treatments incorporate local ingredients such as volcanic mud, sea salt, and aromatic herbs, which are known for their therapeutic properties.

- **Signature Experiences**: Some spas offer signature experiences that are unique to Lipari. For example, volcanic stone massages harness the island's geothermal energy to relieve tension and promote deep relaxation. Another popular treatment is the seaweed wrap, which nourishes the skin and helps detoxify the body.

Wellness Centers Offering Holistic Programs

For those looking for a more immersive wellness experience, several centers in Lipari offer holistic programs that combine various elements of wellness, including physical activity, nutrition, and relaxation.

- **Personalized Wellness Plans**: Wellness centers often provide personalized programs tailored to individual needs. Whether you're looking to lose weight, detox, or simply de-stress, these programs can include a mix of fitness activities, such as yoga or Pilates, healthy meal plans, and a series of spa treatments.
- **Mind-Body Connection**: Many wellness centers emphasize the mind-body connection, offering activities such as guided meditation, mindfulness sessions, and breathwork classes. These practices help guests cultivate a sense of inner peace and mental clarity, complementing the physical benefits of the spa treatments.

Natural Hot Springs and Thermal Baths

The volcanic origins of Lipari and the surrounding Aeolian Islands have endowed the region with natural hot springs and thermal baths that are rich in minerals. These natural spa facilities are perfect for those who want to experience the island's therapeutic offerings in a more rustic, yet equally relaxing, setting.

- **Thermal Baths**: The thermal baths are infused with minerals like sulfur, magnesium, and calcium, which are believed to have healing properties. Bathing in these waters can help alleviate conditions such as arthritis, skin disorders, and respiratory issues, as well as provide general relaxation.
- **Mud Baths**: Another popular natural treatment is the volcanic mud bath, where guests can cover themselves in warm mud rich in minerals before rinsing off in the thermal waters. This practice is known to detoxify the skin, improve circulation, and relieve muscle pain.

Day Spas for Quick Retreats

If you're short on time but still want to enjoy a bit of pampering, Lipari offers several day spas that provide quick yet effective treatments. These spas are perfect for travelers who want to rejuvenate after a day of exploring the island or before heading off on the next leg of their journey.

- **Express Treatments**: Day spas offer a range of express treatments, such as 30-minute massages, mini facials, and revitalizing foot baths. These quick sessions are designed to refresh and invigorate, making them ideal for those on the go.

- **Relaxation Lounges**: Many day spas feature relaxation lounges where you can unwind before or after your treatment. These lounges often have a calming ambiance, with soft lighting, soothing music, and herbal teas to help you fully relax.

Wellness Retreats and Yoga Centers

For those who wish to dive deeper into their wellness journey, Lipari is home to several retreats and yoga centers that offer multi-day programs. These retreats often combine elements of yoga, meditation, healthy eating, and spa treatments to create a comprehensive wellness experience.

- **Yoga Retreats**: Yoga retreats in Lipari are often held in beautiful, serene locations, allowing participants to practice yoga in harmony with nature. Sessions may take place on the beach at sunrise, in lush gardens, or even on terraces overlooking the sea. The retreats usually cater to all levels, from beginners to advanced practitioners.
- **Detox Retreats**: Detox retreats focus on cleansing the body through a combination of healthy eating, spa treatments, and gentle exercise. Participants are guided through a program that may include juice fasting, herbal teas, and detoxifying treatments like lymphatic drainage massages and body wraps.

Local Ingredients and Sustainable Practices

A unique aspect of Lipari's wellness offerings is the emphasis on using local, natural ingredients in treatments. Many spas pride themselves on sourcing ingredients from the island and surrounding regions, ensuring that treatments are both effective and environmentally friendly.

- **Volcanic Ingredients**: Volcanic clay and pumice from the island are commonly used in exfoliating treatments and masks due to their ability to detoxify and purify the skin.
- **Aromatic Herbs**: Local herbs, such as rosemary, lavender, and lemon balm, are often used in aromatherapy treatments to enhance relaxation and provide therapeutic benefits.
- **Sustainability**: Several wellness centers in Lipari are committed to sustainable practices, using eco-friendly products and reducing their environmental impact. This commitment to sustainability adds another layer of mindfulness to your wellness experience.

Lipari's spas and wellness centers offer a wide range of options for relaxation and rejuvenation. Whether you're looking to indulge in luxurious spa treatments, experience the natural healing properties of the island, or embark on a holistic wellness retreat, Lipari provides the perfect setting for nurturing both body and mind.

Relaxing Beaches and Secluded Coves in Lipari

Lipari is a paradise for beach lovers and those seeking tranquil escapes by the sea. The island's coastline is dotted with stunning beaches and hidden coves, each offering a unique experience, from soft sandy shores to rugged volcanic landscapes

Spiaggia di Canneto

Spiaggia di Canneto is one of Lipari's most popular beaches, known for its long stretch of pebble shore and clear, azure waters. Located just a short distance from the main town, Canneto offers a blend of relaxation and convenience, making it a favorite spot for both locals and visitors.

- **Beach Amenities**: Canneto Beach is well-equipped with sunbeds, umbrellas, and beachside cafes where you can enjoy a refreshing drink or a light meal. The calm waters are perfect for swimming, making it a great spot for families with children.
- **Activities**: In addition to sunbathing and swimming, visitors can rent pedal boats, kayaks, or paddleboards to explore the coastline. The beach is also a popular spot for snorkeling, with plenty of marine life to discover just off the shore.
- **Evening Strolls**: As the day draws to a close, the beach transforms into a romantic spot for evening strolls along the water's edge, with the lights of Lipari town twinkling in the distance.

Spiaggia Bianca

Spiaggia Bianca, or White Beach, is famous for its striking white pumice sand and crystal-clear waters. This beach, located on the northeastern coast of the island, is a visual treat and one of the most photogenic spots in Lipari.

- **Unique Landscape**: The white pumice sand gives the beach its distinctive appearance, creating a stunning contrast with the turquoise waters. The beach is surrounded by steep cliffs, adding to its dramatic beauty.
- **Swimming and Snorkeling**: The shallow, calm waters of Spiaggia Bianca are ideal for swimming and snorkeling. The clarity of the water makes it easy to see the colorful fish and marine life that inhabit the area.

- **Access and Seclusion**: While Spiaggia Bianca is one of Lipari's most beautiful beaches, it remains relatively quiet compared to others. The beach is accessible by boat or a steep path from the road above, which helps to keep it less crowded, offering a more secluded experience.

Acquacalda Beach

Located on the northern coast of Lipari, Acquacalda Beach is known for its serene atmosphere and stunning volcanic backdrop. This beach is perfect for those looking to escape the busier spots and enjoy a more tranquil setting.

- **Volcanic Landscape**: Acquacalda Beach is set against the dramatic backdrop of the island's volcanic landscape. The black sand and pebbles, formed from volcanic ash, create a striking contrast with the blue sea.
- **Relaxation**: The beach is less frequented by tourists, making it a peaceful spot to relax and soak up the sun. The quiet atmosphere is perfect for reading, meditating, or simply enjoying the sound of the waves.
- **Sunset Views**: Acquacalda is also known for its breathtaking sunsets. As the sun dips below the horizon, the sky and sea are bathed in hues of orange and pink, providing a stunning natural spectacle.

Secluded Coves: Hidden Gems for Solitude Seekers

Beyond the more accessible beaches, Lipari is home to several secluded coves that offer privacy and solitude. These hidden gems are perfect for travelers looking to escape the crowds and connect with nature in a more intimate setting.

- **Cala del Fico**: This small, rocky cove is one of Lipari's best-kept secrets. Accessible only by boat or a challenging hike, Cala del Fico offers complete seclusion and unspoiled beauty. The clear waters are ideal for snorkeling, and the surrounding cliffs provide a perfect backdrop for a day of relaxation.
- **Cala Junco**: Located on the neighboring island of Panarea, Cala Junco is often visited by those on boat tours from Lipari. This natural swimming pool is surrounded by steep cliffs, creating a sheltered, tranquil environment. The turquoise waters and the stunning rock formations make it a favorite spot for swimming and snorkeling.
- **Valle Muria**: On the western side of Lipari, Valle Muria is a quiet, pebbled beach accessible via a steep path or by boat. The beach is flanked by high cliffs and offers incredible views of the surrounding islands. It's a perfect spot for those who prefer a more adventurous beach experience, with the reward of a serene and beautiful setting.

Porticello

Porticello Beach, located near the former pumice quarries, is another hidden gem on Lipari. The area's history and its unique landscape make it a fascinating spot for those interested in both relaxation and exploration.

- **Historical Landscape**: The white pumice cliffs that once supported a thriving quarrying industry now stand as a testament to Lipari's volcanic past. The remnants of this

history, combined with the beach's natural beauty, create a unique atmosphere.
- **Peaceful Surroundings**: Porticello is relatively quiet, making it an ideal spot for those looking to relax away from the more crowded beaches. The shallow waters are perfect for wading and swimming, and the beach offers plenty of space to spread out and enjoy the sun.

Coral Beach

Coral Beach is a family-friendly beach located near Canneto. Known for its calm waters and soft, sandy shore, it's an excellent choice for travelers with children.

- **Safe Swimming**: The beach's shallow waters are ideal for young swimmers, and the gentle waves make it a safe and enjoyable spot for families to relax.
- **Facilities and Amenities**: Coral Beach is well-equipped with amenities, including sunbeds, umbrellas, and a nearby café where you can grab a bite to eat. The beach's proximity to Canneto town also means that other services, such as restaurants and shops, are just a short walk away.
- **Play Areas**: In addition to its natural beauty, Coral Beach offers play areas and activities for children, ensuring that the whole family can enjoy a fun and relaxing day by the sea.

Practical Tips for Enjoying Lipari's Beaches and Coves

- **Getting There**: While some beaches, like Spiaggia di Canneto and Coral Beach, are easily accessible by foot or car, others, such as Cala del Fico and Spiaggia Bianca, may

require a boat ride or a hike. Consider renting a scooter or a boat to explore the more remote spots.
- **What to Bring**: Many of Lipari's beaches are natural and undeveloped, so it's a good idea to bring essentials like water, snacks, sunscreen, and a hat. For more secluded coves, pack a picnic and enjoy a day away from the crowds.
- **Respecting Nature**: Lipari's beaches and coves are part of its natural heritage, so it's important to respect the environment. Always take your trash with you, avoid disturbing wildlife, and be mindful of the delicate marine ecosystem when snorkeling or swimming.

Lipari's diverse range of beaches and coves offers something for everyone, from lively, amenity-rich spots to secluded, natural hideaways. Whether you're looking to relax in the sun, explore the underwater world, or simply enjoy the beauty of the island's coastline, Lipari's shores provide the perfect setting for an unforgettable seaside experience.

PRACTICAL INFORMATION FOR VISITING LIPARI

When planning a trip to Lipari, having the right practical information can make your visit smoother and more enjoyable. From understanding the local customs to knowing what to pack, a little preparation goes a long way. Here's an overview of essential details to keep in mind for a hassle-free experience on this beautiful Aeolian island.

Language and Communication

The official language spoken in Lipari is Italian. While many locals, especially those working in tourism, understand and speak some English, it's helpful to know a few basic Italian phrases. This can make everyday interactions, such as ordering food or asking for directions, more comfortable and appreciated by the locals.

Currency and Payments

Italy uses the Euro (€) as its currency. ATMs are available in the main town, and most hotels, restaurants, and shops accept credit and debit cards. However, it's advisable to carry some cash, especially if you plan to visit more remote areas or smaller establishments where card payments may not be accepted.

Time Zone

Lipari, like the rest of Italy, operates on Central European Time (CET) during standard time and Central European Summer Time (CEST) during daylight saving time. Make sure to adjust your watch or phone if you're coming from a different time zone.

Electricity and Plug Type

The standard voltage in Lipari is 230V, with a frequency of 50Hz. The plugs used are Type C, F, and L. If you're traveling from a country with different plug types, be sure to bring a suitable adapter to charge your devices.

Emergency Contacts

In case of emergency, the general European emergency number 112 can be dialed for immediate assistance. Lipari also has local police (Carabinieri), medical services, and a small hospital in the main town. It's a good idea to have the contact information for your country's embassy or consulate in Italy as well.

Internet and Connectivity

Wi-Fi is widely available in hotels, cafes, and restaurants in Lipari, but the quality and speed can vary, especially in more remote areas. If you need reliable internet access throughout your trip, consider getting a local SIM card or using an international roaming plan.

Local Etiquette

Respecting local customs and traditions is important in Lipari. Dress modestly when visiting religious sites, and remember that greetings like "Buongiorno" (Good morning) and "Buonasera" (Good evening) are appreciated. Tipping is not obligatory, but it's customary to round up the bill or leave small change in restaurants.

Health and Safety Precautions

Lipari is generally a safe destination, but it's still wise to take standard travel precautions. Keep your belongings secure, particularly in crowded areas. The island's medical facilities can handle most emergencies, but for serious conditions, evacuation to a larger hospital on the mainland might be necessary. Travel insurance that covers health and evacuation is recommended.

Transportation on the Island

Lipari offers various transportation options, including buses, taxis, and rental cars or scooters. Walking is also a great way to explore the island, especially in the main town. If you plan to visit neighboring islands, regular ferry services operate from the main port.

Climate Considerations

The Mediterranean climate in Lipari means hot summers and mild winters. During the summer months, light, breathable clothing is essential, along with sun protection like hats and sunscreen. In the cooler months, layering is key, as temperatures can fluctuate, especially in the evenings.

Local Customs and Traditions

Understanding and respecting local customs can enhance your experience in Lipari. For example, the afternoon siesta is still observed in many places, with shops and businesses closing for a few hours. Planning your day around this can help avoid any inconvenience.

Tipping Guidelines

Tipping in Lipari is typically not expected, but it's always appreciated. In restaurants, rounding up the bill or leaving a small tip for good service is customary. For other services, like taxis or hotel staff, a small tip can be given for exceptional service.

By keeping these practical tips in mind, you'll be well-prepared to enjoy everything Lipari has to offer, making your stay both pleasant and memorable.

Language Tips and Common Phrases

Lipari is part of Italy, so the primary language spoken is Italian. While many locals working in tourism may speak some English, knowing a few basic Italian phrases can enhance your interactions and help you navigate daily activities more smoothly.

- **Basic Greetings**:
    - **Buongiorno** (bwohn-jor-noh) - Good morning
    - **Buonasera** (bwoh-nah-seh-rah) - Good evening
    - **Ciao** (chow) - Hi/Hello (informal)
    - **Arrivederci** (ah-ree-veh-DEHR-chee) - Goodbye
- **Polite Expressions**:
    - **Per favore** (pehr fah-VOH-reh) - Please
    - **Grazie** (GRAHT-see-eh) - Thank you
    - **Prego** (PREH-goh) - You're welcome/Please (offering something)
    - **Mi scusi** (mee SKOO-zee) - Excuse me (for getting someone's attention)

- **Asking for Help**:
    - **Dove si trova ...?** (DOH-veh see TROH-vah) - Where is ...?
        - **Dove si trova la farmacia?** - Where is the pharmacy?
        - **Dove si trova la fermata dell'autobus?** - Where is the bus stop?
    - **Ho bisogno di aiuto** (oh bee-SOH-nyoh dee ah-YOO-toh) - I need help
    - **Parla inglese?** (PAHR-lah een-GLAY-zeh) - Do you speak English?
- **Dining and Shopping**:
    - **Il conto, per favore** (eel KOHN-toh pehr fah-VOH-reh) - The check, please
    - **Quanto costa?** (KWAHN-toh KOH-stah) - How much does it cost?
    - **Che ore sono?** (keh OH-reh SOH-noh) - What time is it?
- **Directions and Transportation**:
    - **Dove si trova ...?** (DOH-veh see TROH-vah) - Where is ...?
        - **Dove si trova la stazione dei treni?** - Where is the train station?
    - **Quanto tempo ci vuole per ...?** (KWAHN-toh TEM-poh chee VOH-leh pehr) - How long does it take to ...?
        - **Quanto tempo ci vuole per arrivare a Lipari?** - How long does it take to get to Lipari?

- **Health and Emergencies**:
    - **Ho bisogno di un medico** (oh bee-SOH-nyoh dee oon MEH-dee-koh) - I need a doctor
    - **Dove si trova l'ospedale?** (DOH-veh see TROH-vah LOH-speh-DAH-leh) - Where is the hospital?

Additional Tips

- **Learn Key Phrases**: Familiarize yourself with these basic phrases before your trip. Even if your Italian isn't perfect, locals will appreciate your effort to communicate in their language.
- **Use Language Apps**: Consider downloading translation apps on your phone for quick assistance with more complex conversations or phrases.
- **Carry a Phrasebook**: A small Italian phrasebook can be handy for reference during your travels.

Having this practical information at hand ensures that you're prepared for any situation that may arise during your visit to Lipari. It can help you navigate local services, enhance your interactions with residents, and ensure a smoother, more enjoyable travel experience.

Useful Websites and Resources

Online Maps and Navigation Apps

- Make use of online maps like Google Maps or Maps.me to navigate the Lipari effortlessly. Be sure to download offline maps for regions with limited internet access, allowing you to explore the city's streets, attractions, and neighborhoods with ease.

Tour Operator Websites

- Research and book tours through reputable tour operators. Websites like **GetYourGuide, Viator, or local operators' official sites** offer various excursions, ensuring a well-organized and enjoyable exploration of Lipari attractions.

Weather Updates

- Stay informed about Lipari weather conditions through reliable weather websites or apps like AccuWeather. This ensures you pack appropriately and plan outdoor activities on days with favorable weather.

Language Learning Resources

To facilitate communication and enhance your cultural immersion, consider language learning resources

- **Duolingo** (www.duolingo.com)**:** A popular language-learning app.
- **Google Translate**: Google Translate can be incredibly helpful for interacting with locals who might not speak English. This free translation app enables real-time translation of both text and speech. It's an excellent tool for engaging with residents and navigating the city. Additionally, you can use the app to photograph signs or menus and get instant translations. For offline access, download the Italian language pack to facilitate easier communication with locals.

However, keep in mind that machine translations like Google Translate are not always perfect, and there may be nuances in language or culture that the app may not fully capture.

Hotel/Accommodation Booking Platforms

- Use reputable booking platforms such as **Booking.com**, **Airbnb**, or **Expedia** to secure accommodation. Read reviews, compare prices, and choose lodgings that align with your preferences and budget.

TripAdvisor (tripadvisor.com)

- Plan and book accommodations, restaurants, and activities based on traveler reviews.

- Access travel forums for advice and tips from experienced travelers.

Hotel or Accommodation Front Desk

Your hotel or accommodation's front desk can provide assistance with various inquiries, including arranging transportation, booking tours or excursions, and addressing any concerns during your stay.

ITINERARIES AND SUGGESTED ROUTES FOR EXPLORING LIPARI

When visiting Lipari, having a well-planned itinerary can help you make the most of your time on the island. Whether you're staying for a day or several, there are various routes and plans that cater to different interests, from historical exploration to nature walks. Here's a guide to some suggested itineraries that will ensure you experience the best of Lipari.

1-Day Itinerary: Highlights of Lipari

If you have just one day to explore the enchanting island of Lipari, this itinerary is designed to ensure you experience the island's most iconic and captivating spots. From historical sites to stunning natural beauty, this guide will help you make the most of your limited time on Lipari.

Morning: Dive into History and Culture

- **Lipari Castle and Museo Archeologico Regionale Eoliano**
    - Begin your day with a visit to **Lipari Castle**, a historical fortress that has stood watch over the island for centuries. Located on a hilltop, the castle offers panoramic views of the surrounding area, making it an ideal starting point for your exploration. Within the castle grounds, you'll find the **Museo Archeologico Regionale Eoliano**, one of the most significant archaeological museums in Italy. The museum houses an impressive collection of artifacts from the Aeolian Islands, including

ancient pottery, tools, and even shipwrecks. Spend the morning wandering through the museum's exhibits to gain insight into the island's rich history, from prehistoric times to the Roman and Byzantine eras.

- **Stroll through the Old Town (Centro Storico)**
    - After your historical tour, take a leisurely stroll through the **Centro Storico** of Lipari. The old town is a maze of narrow streets lined with colorful buildings, charming shops, and lively cafes. As you explore, you'll encounter beautiful churches, such as the **Cathedral of San Bartolomeo**, the island's main religious site. Take your time to enjoy the vibrant atmosphere, perhaps stopping for a coffee or a pastry at one of the local bakeries.

Midday: Savor Local Flavors

- **Lunch at a Traditional Sicilian Restaurant**
    - By midday, you'll likely be ready for a meal. Lipari offers a variety of dining options that showcase the flavors of Sicilian and Aeolian cuisine. Head to a traditional restaurant in the town center, where you can sample local specialties such as **pasta alla Norma**, **caponata**, and fresh seafood dishes. Pair your meal with a glass of **Malvasia** wine, a sweet and aromatic wine produced in the Aeolian Islands.

Afternoon: Relax and Enjoy the Scenery

- **Relax at Spiaggia di Canneto**
    - After lunch, it's time to unwind by the sea. **Spiaggia di Canneto**, one of Lipari's most popular

beaches, is just a short drive or bus ride from the town center. The beach is known for its clear turquoise waters and smooth pebbles, making it a perfect spot for swimming and sunbathing. If you're feeling more adventurous, you can rent a kayak or paddleboard to explore the coastline. Take in the views of the surrounding hills and nearby islands as you relax in the sun.

- **Visit Quattrocchi Viewpoint**
    - Before the day ends, make sure to visit the **Quattrocchi Viewpoint**, one of the island's most breathtaking spots. The viewpoint offers stunning panoramic views of the rugged coastline, the blue waters of the Tyrrhenian Sea, and the nearby island of **Vulcano** with its distinctive smoking crater. This is also a fantastic spot for photography, so be sure to capture the beauty of Lipari from this vantage point.

Evening: Enjoy a Seaside Dinner

- **Dinner with a View**
    - As the sun begins to set, head back to Lipari town for dinner at one of the seaside restaurants. Many establishments offer outdoor seating with views of the harbor, where you can watch the boats come and go as you dine. Enjoy a meal of fresh fish, grilled vegetables, and other local delicacies, all prepared with the simple yet flavorful ingredients that characterize Aeolian cuisine. Finish your meal with a dessert of **granita** or a slice of **cassata**, accompanied by a shot of **limoncello** or **Malvasia**.

Late Evening: Stroll Along the Waterfront

- **Evening Walk and Nightcap**
    - End your day with a leisurely stroll along the waterfront. The harbor area is beautifully lit at night, creating a romantic atmosphere perfect for an evening walk. If you're in the mood, stop by one of the local bars for a nightcap, perhaps enjoying a glass of wine or a cocktail as you reflect on your day exploring Lipari.

This one-day itinerary is designed to give you a taste of Lipari's rich history, vibrant culture, and stunning natural beauty.

3-Day Itinerary: A Deeper Exploration of Lipari

A three-day visit to Lipari allows you to delve deeper into the island's history, culture, and natural beauty. This itinerary is crafted to provide a well-rounded experience, from ancient ruins and picturesque villages to serene beaches and culinary delights.

Day 1: Historical and Cultural Immersion

Morning: Unveil Lipari's Past

- **Lipari Castle and Museo Archeologico Regionale Eoliano**
    - Begin your exploration at **Lipari Castle**, a hilltop fortress that offers a commanding view of the island. Within its walls lies the **Museo Archeologico Regionale Eoliano**, where you can explore a vast collection of artifacts that tell the story of the Aeolian Islands from prehistoric times

to the Roman period. Spend your morning immersing yourself in the island's rich history, wandering through exhibits that include ancient pottery, tools, and shipwrecks.

Midday: Discover the Heart of Lipari

- **Lunch in the Old Town (Centro Storico)**
    - After your museum visit, head down to the **Centro Storico**, Lipari's charming old town. Here, narrow streets are lined with pastel-colored buildings, local boutiques, and bustling cafes. Choose a traditional Sicilian restaurant for lunch, where you can enjoy dishes like **pasta alla Norma** or **insalata di mare**. Afterward, take a leisurely stroll through the streets, stopping by the **Cathedral of San Bartolomeo** and other historic churches.

Afternoon: Experience Lipari's Natural Beauty

- **Scenic Hike to Quattrocchi Viewpoint**
    - In the afternoon, set out on a scenic hike to the **Quattrocchi Viewpoint**. This trail offers breathtaking views of the island's dramatic coastline, with cliffs plunging into the azure sea and the neighboring island of **Vulcano** in the distance. The hike is relatively easy and well-marked, making it accessible for most visitors. Take your time to savor the panoramic views and snap some photos.

Evening: Embrace Lipari's Nightlife

- **Dinner and Evening Stroll**

- o As the day winds down, enjoy dinner at a waterfront restaurant in Lipari town. Many establishments offer outdoor seating with views of the harbor, where you can watch the sun set over the sea. After dinner, take an evening stroll along the waterfront, where the gentle sea breeze and twinkling lights create a perfect ending to your first day.

Day 2: Island Exploration and Coastal Adventures

Morning: Island Hopping and Marine Adventures

- **Boat Tour to Neighboring Islands**
  - o Dedicate your second day to exploring the nearby islands. Start with a boat tour that takes you to **Vulcano** and **Salina**. On Vulcano, you can hike to the top of the active crater for an unparalleled view, or relax in the therapeutic mud baths and hot springs. Afterward, sail to **Salina**, known as the "green island" for its lush landscapes. Here, you can visit local vineyards, hike to the top of **Monte Fossa delle Felci**, or simply enjoy the tranquil beaches.

Midday: Picnic or Lunch on the Islands

- **Seaside Lunch**
  - o During your island hopping, enjoy a picnic by the sea or have lunch at a quaint restaurant on Salina. Sample the local produce, such as **capers** and

Malvasia wine, and savor fresh seafood dishes that highlight the island's culinary traditions.

Afternoon: Relax and Unwind

- **Afternoon at the Beach**
    - Return to Lipari in the afternoon and spend some time relaxing at **Spiaggia di Canneto** or another nearby beach. The calm waters and stunning surroundings make it an ideal spot to unwind after a day of adventure. You might also opt for a kayaking session or a paddleboarding experience to explore the coastline from the water.

Evening: A Taste of Lipari's Culinary Delights

- **Gourmet Dining Experience**
    - For dinner, treat yourself to a gourmet meal at one of Lipari's top restaurants. Try **pesce spada alla ghiotta** (swordfish stew) or **arancini**, paired with local wines. If you're in the mood, enjoy a glass of sweet **Malvasia** as a digestif.

Day 3: Cultural Immersion and Local Flavors

Morning: Explore Lipari's Villages

- **Visit Quattropani and Pianoconte**
    - On your final day, venture out to explore some of Lipari's charming villages. Start with **Quattropani**, located on the western side of the island, known for its stunning views of Salina and the serene **Chiesa**

Vecchia. Then head to **Pianoconte**, a rural village surrounded by vineyards and olive groves. Here, you can visit the **Terme di San Calogero**, ancient thermal baths that date back to the Roman era.

Midday: Farm-to-Table Lunch

- **Lunch in the Countryside**
  - Enjoy a farm-to-table lunch at a local agriturismo in Pianoconte, where you can savor dishes made from fresh, locally-sourced ingredients. This is a great opportunity to taste traditional Aeolian cuisine, including homemade bread, cheese, and seasonal vegetables.

Afternoon: Dive into Lipari's Craft Scene

- **Explore Local Markets and Artisan Shops**
  - In the afternoon, return to Lipari town and spend some time exploring local markets and artisan shops. Look for unique souvenirs, such as handmade ceramics, local wines, and products made from the island's famous capers. Visit the **Ecomuseo della Memoria**, a small museum dedicated to preserving the island's cultural heritage, or browse through galleries showcasing the work of local artists.

Evening: Sunset Cruise and Farewell Dinner

- **Sunset Cruise**
  - As your final evening approaches, embark on a sunset cruise around the island. The golden light of

the setting sun creates a magical atmosphere as you sail past the cliffs and beaches of Lipari. This is the perfect way to reflect on your time on the island.
- **Farewell Dinner**
    - After the cruise, enjoy a farewell dinner at one of Lipari's upscale restaurants. Savor the flavors of your favorite dishes from your trip, and perhaps try something new, like **tonno alla Liparota** (Lipari-style tuna) or **cassatina** for dessert.

This three-day itinerary is designed to give you a comprehensive experience of Lipari, blending history, culture, nature, and culinary delights.

7-Day Itinerary: The Ultimate Lipari Experience

Spending a full week on Lipari allows you to fully immerse yourself in the island's history, culture, natural beauty, and local lifestyle. This seven-day itinerary is designed to provide a balanced mix of exploration, relaxation, and adventure, giving you a true taste of everything Lipari has to offer.

Day 1: Arrival and Initial Exploration

Morning: Arrival and Settling In

- **Arrive on Lipari**
    - Begin your Lipari adventure by arriving on the island, whether by ferry from Sicily or another Aeolian Island. Once you've checked into your accommodation, take a moment to relax and soak in the atmosphere.

Afternoon: Orientation and Initial Exploration

- **Explore Lipari Town**
    - Start your trip with a leisurely walk through **Lipari Town**, the island's vibrant hub. Stroll through the **Centro Storico**, exploring its charming streets, colorful buildings, and local shops. Visit the **Cathedral of San Bartolomeo**, the island's main church, and enjoy your first taste of Aeolian cuisine at a local restaurant for lunch.

Evening: Sunset Stroll

- **Waterfront Walk**
    - End your first day with a walk along the waterfront, enjoying the views of the harbor as the sun sets. This is a perfect introduction to the island's relaxed pace and natural beauty.

Day 2: Dive into History and Culture

Morning: Historical Exploration

- **Lipari Castle and Museo Archeologico Regionale Eoliano**
    - Spend your morning delving into the island's history at **Lipari Castle**. Explore the **Museo Archeologico Regionale Eoliano**, where you'll discover a vast collection of artifacts that trace the island's history from prehistoric times through the Roman era. The museum offers a fascinating insight into the ancient cultures that once thrived on Lipari.

Afternoon: Cultural Immersion

- **Visit to Quattropani and the Chiesa Vecchia**
  - After lunch, venture to **Quattropani**, a picturesque village on the western side of the island. Visit the **Chiesa Vecchia**, a small church that offers panoramic views of Salina and the Tyrrhenian Sea. The peaceful atmosphere and stunning scenery make it a perfect spot for reflection.

Evening: Traditional Dinner

- **Dinner in Lipari Town**
  - Return to Lipari Town for dinner at a traditional Sicilian restaurant. Enjoy dishes like **pasta alla Norma** and **arancini**, paired with local wines, as you unwind after a day of exploration.

Day 3: Island Adventures and Coastal Beauty

Morning: Island Hopping

- **Boat Tour to Vulcano**
  - Dedicate your third day to exploring the nearby island of **Vulcano**. Take a boat tour that allows you to hike to the crater of the active volcano, where you'll be rewarded with breathtaking views. Alternatively, relax in the island's famous **mud baths** and **hot springs**.

Afternoon: Return to Lipari

- **Relax at Spiaggia di Canneto**
    - After returning to Lipari, spend the afternoon relaxing at **Spiaggia di Canneto**, one of the island's most popular beaches. The crystal-clear waters and pebbly shore provide a perfect spot for swimming and sunbathing.

Evening: Seaside Dining

- **Dinner with a View**
    - Enjoy a seaside dinner at one of the restaurants near Canneto, where you can savor fresh seafood dishes while watching the sunset over the sea.

Day 4: Nature and Outdoor Activities

Morning: Hiking and Scenic Views

- **Hike to Quattrocchi Viewpoint**
    - Start your day with a hike to the **Quattrocchi Viewpoint**, a must-see spot on the island. The trail offers stunning views of the rugged coastline, with cliffs dropping into the turquoise waters below. The viewpoint is also a fantastic spot for photography, so be sure to bring your camera.

Afternoon: Explore Nature Reserves

- **Visit the Valle Muria Beach and Punta della Crapazza**
    - In the afternoon, visit **Valle Muria Beach**, a secluded cove known for its dramatic cliffs and

tranquil waters. Nearby, the **Punta della Crapazza** offers even more stunning views and opportunities for hiking.

Evening: Local Cuisine

- **Dinner at a Traditional Restaurant**
    - Head back to Lipari Town for dinner at a restaurant specializing in Aeolian cuisine. Enjoy dishes made with local ingredients, such as **caponata** and **panelle**, and perhaps try a glass of **Malvasia** wine.

Day 5: Cultural Insights and Relaxation

Morning: Art and Local Crafts

- **Explore Lipari's Artisan Shops and Art Galleries**
    - Spend the morning exploring the artisan shops and galleries in Lipari Town. Look for handmade ceramics, local wines, and other unique souvenirs. Visit the **Ecomuseo della Memoria**, a small museum dedicated to preserving the island's cultural heritage.

Afternoon: Visit to the Terme di San Calogero

- **Thermal Baths**
    - In the afternoon, visit the **Terme di San Calogero** in Pianoconte, ancient thermal baths dating back to Roman times. Enjoy a relaxing soak in the warm waters, which are said to have therapeutic properties.

Evening: Culinary Experience

- **Farm-to-Table Dinner**
    - End your day with a farm-to-table dinner at a local agriturismo, where you can enjoy dishes made with fresh, locally-sourced ingredients. This is a great opportunity to taste traditional Aeolian cuisine in a rustic, authentic setting.

Day 6: Water Activities and Island Exploration

Morning: Snorkeling and Diving

- **Explore Lipari's Underwater World**
    - Dedicate your sixth day to exploring Lipari's underwater world. Join a snorkeling or diving excursion to discover the rich marine life around the island. The crystal-clear waters and diverse ecosystems make Lipari a fantastic destination for underwater exploration.

Afternoon: Island Hopping to Salina

- **Visit to Salina**
    - After your morning in the water, take a boat trip to **Salina**, the greenest of the Aeolian Islands. Explore its lush landscapes, visit a local vineyard, and perhaps hike to the top of **Monte Fossa delle Felci** for breathtaking views.

Evening: Sunset Cruise

- **Sunset Sailing**
  - Return to Lipari in the evening for a sunset cruise around the island. The golden light of the setting sun creates a magical atmosphere, making this a perfect way to end your day.

Day 7: Final Day of Exploration and Reflection

Morning: Relax and Unwind

- **Visit to a Secluded Cove**
  - On your final day, take it easy with a visit to one of Lipari's secluded coves, such as **Spiaggia Bianca** or **Acquacalda Beach**. Spend your morning relaxing by the sea, taking in the tranquility of the island's less-visited spots.

Afternoon: Last-Minute Shopping

- **Explore Local Markets**
  - In the afternoon, return to Lipari Town for some last-minute shopping. Visit the local markets to pick up any souvenirs you might have missed, such as local wines, ceramics, or artisanal foods.

Evening: Farewell Dinner

- **Final Meal on Lipari**
  - End your Lipari adventure with a farewell dinner at one of the island's top restaurants. Savor your favorite dishes from the trip, perhaps enjoying a

final glass of **Malvasia** as you reflect on your week-long exploration of this beautiful island.

This seven-day itinerary provides a comprehensive experience of Lipari, allowing you to immerse yourself in its history, culture, natural beauty, and local lifestyle. By the end of your trip, you'll have a deep appreciation for the unique charm and allure of Lipari, making it a destination you'll remember long after you've left.

Special Interest Itineraries: Tailored Experiences in Lipari

Lipari offers a diverse range of experiences, catering to travelers with various interests, from history buffs to nature lovers and culinary enthusiasts. These special interest itineraries are designed to provide a deep dive into specific aspects of the island, allowing you to tailor your visit to your passions.

History and Culture Itinerary

Day 1: Ancient Beginnings

- **Museo Archeologico Regionale Eoliano**: Start your historical journey at the **Museo Archeologico Regionale Eoliano**, where you can explore artifacts from the Neolithic era to the Roman period. The museum's collection offers a comprehensive overview of the island's long and fascinating history.
- **Lipari Castle**: After the museum, head to **Lipari Castle**, where you can walk through the ancient walls and enjoy panoramic views of the town and the sea. The castle, which

has stood for centuries, provides a tangible connection to the island's past.

Day 2: Religious Heritage

- **Cathedral of San Bartolomeo**: Visit the island's main church, dedicated to **San Bartolomeo**, the patron saint of Lipari. The cathedral's baroque architecture and religious artifacts offer insight into the island's spiritual history.
- **Chiesa Vecchia in Quattropani**: In the afternoon, travel to the **Chiesa Vecchia** in Quattropani, a small, historic church with stunning views. This site is perfect for reflecting on the religious and cultural significance of Lipari.

Day 3: Exploring Villages and Traditions

- **Villages of Pianoconte and Canneto**: Spend the day visiting traditional villages like **Pianoconte** and **Canneto**. Here, you'll find local crafts, traditional architecture, and a slower pace of life that reflects Lipari's rich cultural heritage.
- **Ecomuseo della Memoria**: End your historical exploration at the **Ecomuseo della Memoria**, a museum that preserves the island's intangible cultural heritage, including its maritime traditions and folklore.

Nature and Adventure Itinerary

Day 1: Coastal Wonders

- **Boat Tour Around Lipari**: Begin your adventure with a boat tour around Lipari, where you can explore the island's rugged coastline, hidden coves, and sea caves. The tour

offers opportunities for swimming, snorkeling, and appreciating the island's natural beauty from the water.
- **Spiaggia di Canneto**: In the afternoon, relax at **Spiaggia di Canneto**, a beautiful beach with crystal-clear waters, perfect for unwinding after a morning of exploration.

Day 2: Hiking and Panoramic Views

- **Quattrocchi Viewpoint**: Hike to the **Quattrocchi Viewpoint**, one of the most scenic spots on the island. The trail offers breathtaking views of the coastline and the nearby island of Vulcano, making it a must for nature lovers and photographers.
- **Valle Muria Beach**: Continue your hiking adventure to **Valle Muria Beach**, a secluded cove surrounded by dramatic cliffs. The journey and the destination both provide a sense of connection with nature.

Day 3: Island Hopping

- **Visit to Vulcano**: Take a day trip to **Vulcano**, known for its active volcano and unique landscapes. Hike to the crater for panoramic views, or relax in the island's famous mud baths and hot springs.
- **Return to Lipari**: In the evening, return to Lipari and enjoy a quiet dinner at a restaurant with a view of the sea.

Culinary Exploration Itinerary

Day 1: Introduction to Aeolian Cuisine

- **Cooking Class**: Begin your culinary journey with a cooking class where you'll learn to prepare traditional

Aeolian dishes such as **caponata**, **pasta alla Norma**, and **cassatelle**. This hands-on experience will deepen your appreciation for the island's flavors.
- **Dinner at a Farm-to-Table Restaurant**: In the evening, dine at a farm-to-table restaurant, where you can savor dishes made with fresh, local ingredients. Enjoy a glass of **Malvasia** wine as you take in the island's culinary delights.

Day 2: Vineyard and Wine Tasting

- **Visit to a Local Vineyard**: Spend the day at a vineyard, where you can learn about the wine-making process and sample some of the island's best wines, including the renowned **Malvasia delle Lipari**.
- **Picnic Lunch in the Vineyards**: Enjoy a picnic lunch amidst the vines, featuring local cheeses, olives, and fresh bread, paired with the vineyard's wines.
- **Dinner in Lipari Town**: End the day with dinner at a traditional Sicilian restaurant, where you can taste more of the island's culinary specialties.

Day 3: Market and Street Food Exploration

- **Visit to Lipari's Food Markets**: Start your day at Lipari's bustling food markets, where you can discover local products, from fresh seafood to seasonal fruits and vegetables. This is a great opportunity to taste **pane cunzatu** and other street food.
- **Street Food Tour**: Continue with a street food tour of Lipari Town, sampling dishes like **arancini**, **panelle**, and **granita**. This casual exploration allows you to enjoy the island's flavors on the go.

Art and Craft Itinerary

Day 1: Art Galleries and Artisan Shops

- **Explore Local Art Galleries**: Start your artistic journey by visiting Lipari's art galleries, where you can view works by local and regional artists. The galleries showcase a variety of styles, from traditional to contemporary.
- **Visit Artisan Shops**: Spend the afternoon visiting artisan shops, where you can purchase handmade ceramics, jewelry, and other crafts. These unique pieces make for memorable souvenirs.

Day 2: Creative Workshops

- **Ceramics Workshop**: Participate in a ceramics workshop where you can learn about traditional Aeolian pottery techniques and create your own piece of art to take home.
- **Painting Class**: In the afternoon, join a painting class that takes inspiration from Lipari's landscapes. Whether you're a beginner or an experienced artist, this activity offers a creative way to connect with the island.

Day 3: Cultural Experiences

- **Visit to the Ecomuseo della Memoria**: Spend the day at the **Ecomuseo della Memoria**, where you can learn about the island's cultural heritage, including its crafts and maritime traditions.
- **Attend a Local Festival or Cultural Event**: If your visit coincides with one of Lipari's festivals, such as the **Festa di San Bartolomeo**, take the opportunity to experience the

island's vibrant cultural life. These events often include traditional music, dance, and crafts.

Wellness and Relaxation Itinerary

Day 1: Spa and Wellness Centers

- **Morning at a Spa**: Start your wellness journey with a morning at one of Lipari's spas. Enjoy a range of treatments, from massages to facials, designed to help you relax and rejuvenate.
- **Afternoon Yoga Session**: Participate in a yoga session at a wellness center or on the beach. The calming environment and gentle exercise will help you feel centered and refreshed.

Day 2: Meditation and Nature

- **Meditation Spot at Quattropani**: Spend the morning meditating at the **Chiesa Vecchia** in Quattropani, a peaceful spot with stunning views. The quiet atmosphere and natural beauty make it an ideal place for reflection.
- **Nature Walk at Punta della Crapazza**: In the afternoon, take a nature walk at **Punta della Crapazza**, where the scenic landscapes provide a tranquil setting for relaxation.

Day 3: Relaxing Beaches

- **Visit to Secluded Coves**: Dedicate your final day to visiting Lipari's most secluded beaches, such as **Spiaggia Bianca** or **Acqucalda Beach**. Spend the day swimming, sunbathing, and enjoying the serenity of these hidden gems.

These special interest itineraries offer a focused experience of Lipari, tailored to your unique passions. It doesn't matter if you're interested in history, nature, art, or relaxation, Lipari provides the perfect backdrop for a memorable and enriching vacations

Feel free to adjust the itinerary based on your interests and preferences.

CONCLUSION

As you conclude your journey through Lipari, the largest of the Aeolian Islands, you carry with you the vibrant colors, rich history, and stunning landscapes that make this destination truly unique. From the charming streets of Lipari Town to the breathtaking views atop the ancient castle, every corner of the island offers a blend of natural beauty and cultural heritage.

You've explored the mesmerizing beaches, tasted exquisite local cuisine, and immersed yourself in the traditions and warmth of the island's people. Whether you wandered through the archaeological museum, enjoyed a leisurely boat trip to nearby islands, or savored a sunset over the Tyrrhenian Sea, Lipari has undoubtedly left an indelible mark on your heart.

As you plan your trip to Lipari, keep in mind that this guide is just the beginning. Lipari is a dynamic and ever-changing place, with new attractions and experiences popping up all the time. So don't be afraid to explore beyond the pages of this guidebook and discover the place for yourself.

We hope this guide has provided you with the inspiration and information you need to plan fun activities in Lipari. Whether you're visiting for the first time or returning for a repeat visit, we know you will fall in love with this beautiful destination and all that it has to offer.

ON A FINAL NOTE

The information presented in this travel guide is intended for general informational purposes, and considerable effort has been exerted to ensure the accuracy of the information. Readers are urged to exercise their discretion and take responsibility for their own travel decisions and activities when implementing the suggestions and recommendations found in this guide. Please be aware that details such as prices, operational hours, and other specifics are subject to change without prior notice. It is advisable to verify this information with relevant authorities, businesses, or organizations before finalizing any travel plans or reservations.

It is essential to clarify that the mention of particular products, services, businesses, or organizations in this guide does not imply an endorsement by the author. Readers are strongly encouraged to observe necessary precautions and adhere to local laws, regulations, and customs. The author and publisher of this travel guide disclaim any responsibility for inaccuracies or omissions and disclaim liability for any potential damages or losses resulting from the application of the information provided herein.

Thank you for choosing this guide, until we meet again on another adventure.

MY JOURNAL

....
....
....
....
....
....
....
....
....
....
....
....
....
....
....
....
....

Made in the USA
Las Vegas, NV
11 May 2025